INVESTIGATING
ORGANISED
CRIME
AND WAR CRIMES

INVESTIGATING
ORGANISED CRIME
AND WAR CRIMES

A Personal Account of a Senior Detective in
Kosovo, Iraq and Beyond

Anthony Nott MBE

Pen & Sword
MILITARY

First published in Great Britain in 2017 by
PEN & SWORD MILITARY
an imprint of
Pen & Sword Books Ltd,
47 Church Street,
Barnsley,
South Yorkshire,
S70 2AS

A CIP record for this book is available from the British Library.

ISBN 978 1 47389 891 2

Printed and bound by Gutenberg Press Ltd., Malta

Pen & Sword Books Ltd incorporates the Imprints of Pen & Sword Aviation, Pen & Sword Maritime, Pen & Sword Military, Wharncliffe Local History, Pen & Sword Select, Pen & Sword Military Classics and Leo Cooper.

For a complete list of Pen & Sword titles please contact
Pen & Sword Books Limited
47 Church Street, Barnsley, South Yorkshire, S70 2AS, England

E-mail: enquiries@pen-and-sword.co.uk
Website: www.pen-and-sword.co.uk

CONTENTS

Acknowledgements

I would like to thank my sister Patricia Blewett and my neighbour Jim Mason for their advice, clarity of thought and suggestions as to the content and structure of this book. I am deeply indebted to Mrs Ursula Jeffries handing me a boxful of commas to sprinkle liberally throughout the work. I would also like to thank Malcolm Davey and his wife Jan (who is also the Editor of the *Free Portland News*) for their proofreading of these recollections and devoting acres of time to the checking and re-checking of these accounts.

The presentation of the book in its current form would not have been possible without the professional guidance , encouragement and punctilious adherence to English grammar by Carol Trow, herself an accomplished author.

I would also like to thank the friends and former colleagues with whom I served, upon whom I imposed certain sections of the book to double check the accuracy of the accounts related herein. There are also those people caught up in some of these events who I am unable to publicly thank, but wish to acknowledge. Without their assistance and support, I would not have been assured as to the accuracy of all the facts, or confident enough to publish this information to the wider public.

I should also like to thank profusely my wife Judith, who has had to live through these events, putting up with my worries, doubts and frustration, plus my boring her into submission when

I recounted mind-numbing detailed accounts about the ins and outs of matters which occurred in a world she does not understand.

Preface

I started out life as a very innocent youth from Devon, a country boy who was shocked by the reality of the policing which I encountered when I joined the Metropolitan Police in 1971. It was a very different world in those days and I was not ready for some of the practices I came across, nor the evil to which a few people could stoop. I transferred to the county force of Dorset in 1976, which, having just served over six years in the Met, was like landing on another planet. I got to learn the different approach to policing taken in a county police force and spent most of my service as a career detective. I then went on to serve as a senior police advisor in the Balkans and Middle East and it is these experiences on which this book focusses.

I volunteered to lead the British forensic team in Kosovo in 2000, where I was deployed for just under two months. I have recounted the sterling work carried out by British police officers serving on this team and describe the daily tragedies and horror of what they uncovered. However, amongst the misery and brutality of the war crimes committed, I found the triumph of the human spirit in the local people to be humbling and truly inspiring.

I then went on to serve over two years in Bosnia, where I led the UK contingent of police officers who were engaged as part of the UN in rebuilding the police in a country which had been torn apart in a fratricidal civil war. I occupied a key command position as a regional police commander in northern Bosnia and then served on an EU mission as the senior advisor on organised crime. I have described in some depth my dealings in the world of human trafficking, primarily focusing on sexual exploitation. I have related some conflicting rivalries and dynamics encountered when the UN mission handed over to an EU policing mission and illustrate some underhand practices which made me think that some members of the UN mission wished to see the EU fail in this area to the detriment of the victims of these crimes.

Between May 2005 and May 2006, I was the deputy police contingent commander for the UK police in Iraq engaged on training and reform of the Iraqi Police Service. I have detailed some of the successes of the Iraqi police but also highlight the involvement of elements of the Iraq police, in murder for both profit and sectarian reasons. I worked daily at the Ministry of Interior in Baghdad and witnessed the steady and remorseless takeover of the police from its original Sunni base to one that would be dominated by Shia Muslims.

It was a great privilege, as a detective, to be involved in the investigation into the kidnap and murder of Margaret Hassan. She devoted her life to helping the poor and disadvantaged in Palestine and Iraq. When she was kidnapped the UK government maintained its policy of not negotiating with hostage takers and terrorists, which I believe led to missed opportunities. My driving force in writing this book comes from my deep belief that this policy is wrong and I articulate my reasons why; I urge that this policy be re-evaluated.

I then went on to serve for two years working in Israel and Palestine with a US led effort to reform, train and equip the Palestinian security services. A separate EU mission was engaged in working with the Palestinian police and I was the liaison officer between both missions. I am therefore able to describe the under-reported work being carried out by the militaries of the UK, US, and Canada plus that by European police officers in building the capacity of the Palestinian security services. This in turn will enable the Palestinian Authority to combat terrorism, bringing added security to not only their own citizens, but also those of Israel.

Another reason for me to put pen to paper is that I learnt a lot about institution building and the practices of police personnel in different parts of the world. During each mission I increased my knowledge and wish to share some crucial lessons I learned, for example, the importance to establish early what criminal law system operates in the country whose police and institutions you are trying to help. I have also laid out some of the errors I have made, or indeed good and creative ideas by others to provide learning points.

Throughout these missions, I maintained personal diaries kept in accordance with my detective training. I have recounted some conversations in this book in direct speech, which were recorded soon after the events described and when facts were still fresh in my mind. I have also drawn upon case notes and reports I personally compiled for my own use and which helped me navigate my way through myriad unfamiliar names and places.

I have been scrupulous to avoid any reference to anything which may still be classified. Many of the operations I have been involved in were secret, for example the raid on the bunker in Baghdad. But once the operation had taken place and impact dealt with, it becomes a matter of public record and its currency as secret has been passed. Equally, where I have been involved in any investigation, I have recounted only that which became evident at trial or in newspaper reports so as to be in the public domain.

I have used the real names of senior personnel from ambassadors to generals because their roles are a matter of public record. Most police officers were content for me to use their real names; however, in some cases I have obscured the identity of some officers and diplomats, at their request and for reasons of security.

Whilst the subjects contained within this work are immensely serious and deal with untimely death on a sometimes industrial scale, I have adopted a personal approach and any lightness detected in my words are not intended to detract from the misery suffered by many. I just wish to get these first hand eye-witness accounts to a readership so that an intimate understanding of the events recounted will be gained.

Tony Nott
Dorset
2017

Acronyms

BIAP	Baghdad International Airport
BiH	Bosnia and Herzegovina
CPA	Coalition Provisional Authority
CPATT	Civilian Police Assistance Training Team
CPS	Crown Prosecution Service
CRG	Controlled Risks Group
DIFAC	Dining Facility
DFID	Department for International Development (UK Government Department)
DOD	Department of Defence (US)
EFP	Explosively Formed Projectile
EUPM	European Union Police Mission
EUPOLCOPPS	European Union Police Co-ordinating Office for Palestinian Police Support
FRE	Former Regime Elements
FCO	Foreign and Commonwealth Office
FOB	Forward Operating Base
ICITAP	International Criminal Investigative Training and assistance Programme (US Department of Justice)
ICTY	International Criminal Tribunal for the Former Yugoslavia
IDF	Israeli Defence Force
IED	Improvised Explosive Device

ING	Iraqi Army National Guard
IOM	International Organisation for Migration
IPTF	International Police Task Force (UN Bosnia)
IPS/IP	Iraqi Police Service
KLA	Kosovo Liberation Army
MCU	Major Crime Unit (Iraq)
MOI	Ministry of Interior
MNSTC-I	Multi National Security Transition Command – Iraq
OHR	Office of the High Representative
OSCE	Organisation for Security and Co-operation in Europe
PSC	Public Security Centre (Bosnian Serb Police Station)
PSD	Private Security Detail
RMP	Royal Military Police
RS	Republika Srbska
SBS	State Border Service (Bosnia)
SFOR	Stabilisation Force (NATO Bosnia)
SIO	Senior Investigating Officer
SIPA	State Investigation and Protection Agency (Bosnia)
STOP	Special Trafficking Operations Programme (UN)
SVBIED	Suicide Vehicle Born Improvised Explosive Device
UCK	Ushria Clirmtare e Kosoves (Kosovo Liberation Army)
UNICEF	United Nations Children's Fund
UNMIBH	United Nations Mission in Bosnia and Herzegovina
UNODC	United Nations Office on Drugs and Crime
UNOHCHR	United Nations Office of the High Commission for Human Rights
USAID	US Agency for International Development
USSC	United States Security Co-ordinator (Israel / Palestine)

Chapter One
The Ups and Downs of a Detective's Life

In February 1999 I was a detective superintendent in the Dorset Police based at the force headquarters which are located in the centre of the county at Winfrith. This is a very rural location and was a long way from the buzz and excitement of Weymouth, Bournemouth and Poole where I had built my career in the CID. I had twenty-five successful homicide investigations under my belt, I had investigated over a hundred suspicious deaths or suicides and my office wall was covered in certificates of commendation from chief constables and various judges. Together with another detective superintendent, I was responsible for all homicide enquiries, major sensitive investigations and the tricky business of managing informants. Life was good, indeed life was very good – then the phone rang.

The caller introduced himself as a senior investigator with the Criminal Cases Review Commission (CCRC). I was asked if I was involved in the case of Russell Causley, who was convicted of murder at Winchester Crown Court in December of 1996.

With a lump in my throat I said, 'Yes.'

I was told that doubts had arisen over the evidence given by one or two prosecution witnesses at the original trial which may have led to a miscarriage of justice. These were serving prisoners to whom Causley had made admissions regarding his wife's killing while he was in prison awaiting trial for a life insurance fraud. I was asked to preserve all material in the case, including court exhibits and police officers' note books which would then be seized by senior police officers from another force. An independent enquiry would then take place by this new team into the conduct of the Dorset Police and the trial. I had been closely involved in scrutinising the evidence given by these convicted prisoners and if I had failed to test the reliability of their accounts with due diligence then there would be only one person to blame and that was me.

I had become involved in the investigation into Russell Causley when I was the detective chief inspector in Bournemouth during the spring of 1994. It had started out by accident when a detective sergeant from the States of Guernsey Police had come to Bournemouth looking for Causley, who he suspected of a life insurance fraud. He mentioned, almost as an aside, that the suspect had reported his wife as a missing person from the matrimonial home in Bournemouth some eight years earlier. I assigned two of my best detectives to have a look at the missing person report to establish that everything was all right. It turned out that it was anything but all right and over the next two years we were able to put together a case, so convincing that Causley was convicted of his wife's murder by the unanimous verdict of the jury in December 1996. His wife's body was never recovered and when I subsequently went to visit him in prison to ask him what he had done with her he refused to speak to me. Nothing more was heard of the matter until I received the phone call from the CCRC.

With some trepidation I went to see the Deputy Chief Constable, George Pothecary, a pragmatic and hard-nosed policeman who worked in an office one floor beneath mine. As I went through the details of the telephone call, I could see the concern start to grow on his face. The CCRC were established in the 1980s to investigate potential miscarriages of justice following a series of wrongful convictions in that decade. If the CCRC are involved in poking around in a case prosecuted by a police force and the words 'miscarriage of justice' are even hinted at it is a cause for concern and for the senior investigating officer (SIO) even worse news; and I was that SIO. I slunk back to my office full of trepidation. Over the next few months, a team of police officers led by a detective superintendent crawled all over the case and eventually the appeal court ordered that Causley be released from prison to face a fresh trial.

Much later, in March 2004, Russell Causley once again stood trial for the murder of his wife. The defence argued for four days before a jury was sworn in, that he should not have to face a second trial. It was also alleged that he was suffering from signs of post-traumatic stress disorder and depression. The judge did not accept the arguments presented and ordered that the trial proceed. No evidence was heard in relation to Causley's conversations with the disputed witnesses. However, despite this, additional evidence was heard from other witnesses and the jury returned a unanimous verdict (again) of guilty of murder and he was for a second time sentenced to life imprisonment. It was not until 2015 that Causley finally admitted murdering his wife in their house in Bournemouth and disposing of her body.

But none of this was known at the time and a great shadow hung over my integrity. Whilst the re-investigation was taking its deliberate course and just to pile on the grief, I was removed from the CID to a small department called 'Community Safety'. This comprised a dedicated bunch of people who worked on crime prevention and various community projects such as setting up 'youth shelters' in parks to give youngsters somewhere to go. A big project they were undertaking involved a warehouse on an industrial estate, which contained all sorts of displays aimed at educating children about the dangers of crossing the road and climbing down into road works and the like. The chief constable thought I would like my own department (of twelve people!). Call me old fashioned but when I learned that my place on CID was to be taken by a 'Bramshill Flyer', that is a young in-service superintendent who had never been in the CID in his life, but needed to show such experience on his CV before being promoted to assistant chief constable, I became a little cynical. The fact that this person was returning to the force from a secondment to Her Majesty's Inspector of Constabulary, who have great influence on chief constables, would of course have had nothing to do with it! It was clear that I had become toxic and remembered that success has many friends but failure is an orphan.

Before I went completely mad, an urge I had had years before came to fruition. During the late 1990s, my wife and I had become increasingly frustrated by the apparent impotence of the world community to end the bloodletting in the Balkans where we watched nightly on our television screens the slaughter of innocent civilians. In early 2000 I had seen an advertisement in the Dorset Police General Orders inviting applications from superintendents to lead the British Forensic Team in Kosovo to assist with mass grave exhumations. The NATO invasion of Kosovo had taken place nine months earlier and was, it must be said, a brave decision by the then Prime Minister Tony Blair, who had in effect led the International Community to rescue the mainly Moslem Albanian population from genocide. My usual good luck seemed to have deserted me and I didn't get the job. However, in July that year I was in the gym – I had consigned beer and curry as the main off duty exercise of a CID man to the bin years before – when I saw Ian Coombes from the Personnel Department.

'Oh, hello, Tony,' he said. 'The Home Office phoned today to ask if you could take over the British Forensic Team in Kosovo for a couple of months, but I told them you were on leave in August.'

I nearly fainted. I couldn't believe the opportunity to be involved in such an important and world-shattering event had slipped through my fingers.

'Ian, forget my leave, forget everything; I want that job, phone them back now please.'

I was reduced to begging; he abandoned his lunch break and made the call. Then, when he did make the call, the guy dealing with it in the Home Office was at lunch, so it was another agonising wait, but yes, I got the job. Now all I had to do was wheedle round the Deputy Chief Constable, George Pothecary, to let me go. I think he knew I had acted correctly and with propriety in the Causley case and badly needed to be immersed back into the world of major crime so he was willing to release me for a couple of months.

Chapter Two
Kosovo 2000

Marshal Tito had held Yugoslavia together since the end of the Second World War. He was a strong man who managed to blend the disparate nationalities of Serb Croat, Slovenian, Kosovo Albanian, Montenegrin and Bosnian into one nation; Yugoslav or South Slav. He also kept Yugoslavia independent from the Soviet Union and had a special status with the West; this kept his country quite prosperous. However, with his death in 1980 and the fall of the Berlin Wall and Soviet era communism, the old nationalist and religious differences arose again, added to which was more than a sprinkling of naked ambition by certain politicians. Notable amongst these was Slobodan Milosevic, a man who would do anything to gain power and feed his ego. He started in Kosovo in the late 1980s by removing Kosovo Albanians from positions of power and influence, just like Hitler removed the Jews from public positions in the 1930s, and then moved onto the rest of Yugoslavia which he tried to run with ethnic Serbs. The Yugoslav Civil War first erupted in Slovenia, followed by Croatia and Bosnia and did not fully come to an end until NATO invaded Kosovo in 1999. In 1995 the CIA assessed that 90 per cent of the atrocities in the Balkans had been carried out by the Serbs. Many of these were at the hands of violent criminals who had been let out of prison by Milosevic and been formed into paramilitary units. They raped, robbed and murdered non-Serb populations, (mainly Muslims) and it was their handiwork which would occupy me.

I flew out to Kosovo on the 8 August 2000 with a considerable amount of sadness at leaving my wife for the next seven weeks. I did however have a sense of excitement about the job in hand and the importance of it. My task was to be the team leader of the British Forensic Team, which was fully funded by the government as part of its contribution in helping bring peace and stability to the Balkans. The British Forensic Team had been tasked to carry out exhumations of suspected war crimes victims in the Pristina area of Kosovo.

The exhumation team was made up of police exhibits officers, photographers, file builders (documentation) and officers whose job it was to dig up the corpses and recover the remains. As part of the usual police black humour they were referred to internally as subterranean technicians. The team also included civilian forensic anthropologists and pathologists, and radiographers, who were usually part of the armed forces medical services, plus a mortuary technician.

The exhumation team was responsible for liaising with the International Criminal Tribunal for the Former Yugoslavia, (ICTY) who were the lead investigators and from whom we received our directions. Once assigned a map reference, it was the team's duty to carry out the exhumations, follow evidential identification procedures, carry out post mortems and prepare the evidence to support charges of systematic genocide. After the bodies had passed through this process, they were returned to the next of kin, if known, for re-interment. ICTY was staffed by many former retired and seconded UK police officers, who worked under the direction of the prosecutor, Carla Ponte. The team worked in partnership with other agencies, both governmental and non-governmental organisations and included various UN departments. NATO forces were crucial to the success of the whole effort.

I landed at Skopje Airport, Macedonia, to be met by a wall of heat and the rotund frame of Detective Superintendent Steve Watts of the Hampshire Police, who I was to temporarily replace.

He drove me through mountainous tree-lined gorges into the central plain of Kosovo. It immediately led me to believe that if a ground war had been launched by NATO and our troops met with determined resistance from the Serbian army, then it would have been a very bloody business. We arrived in Pristina three hours later at a house where the whole team lived. The pollution in the air was thick – the product of the lack of investment this region had suffered for over ten years since Slobodan Milosevic had deliberately withdrawn funding from Kosovo. A nearby lead factory pumped out enormous clouds of pollution, so much so that pregnant women were barred from serving with international organisations working in this region.

I met the team which was formed of seconded police officers from all over the UK. The three core members were highly experienced officers from South Yorkshire, Northern Ireland and the London Metropolitan Police. These three officers were permanent members of the team, whilst the other specialists rotated in and out every eight weeks. It did take me a few days to convince some of the big city cops that police officers from a rural county like Dorset do deal with more than offences against sheep and one big city cop needed a little help in getting the message. The police and scientific staff blended well together and all worked with total commitment. During my whole trip we only had two days off in seven weeks and we all worked at least ten hours a day.

Over the next two days, Steve Watts bombarded me with names, organisations and procedures which nearly made my brain explode. He also gave me a crash course in Microsoft Excel and helped me open my very first e-mail account. By this time of my career I was used to having my own personal assistant, but there is no such luxury on foreign missions; you have to do everything yourself. I had to run just to stand still and I became accustomed to the sound of AK47 fire most evenings, dubbed 'happy-fire' by the veterans. A gun and vendetta culture existed in this region and homicides in Pristina were frequent during my stay.

After a hot and humid night with little sleep and lots of worry about whether I was up to it, I was awoken by the wail of the muezzin at 5am calling the faithful to prayer. This was also the signal to get up in order to be at the gravesite by 6am. We were engaged in a mass exhumation of sixty-three people buried at Makoc cemetery by relatives. These people had been pulled out of a convoy of refugees in March/April of 1999, robbed and then shot at short range – very short range in many cases. Amongst the dead at Makoc was an eight-year-old girl who had been shot running away from the murderous scene. Her father was also present at the exhumation as he had buried her in a hurry with the other victims in a shallow grave. She had been staying for safety with her uncle, who had survived the murder of a group of fifty villagers and was a witness to the slaughter of his friends and his niece. Why he survived and she didn't I was unable to find out; no doubt this will haunt him until the day he dies.

There was considerable evidence to show that many of the victims had been shot numerous times about the body in a chillingly systematic manner. The killers were believed to be paramilitaries, supposedly Arkan's White Wolves. I attended the mortuary every day which was based in Pristina hospital to ensure that we could cope with the throughput of bodies and maintain the high standard of autopsies. The pathologist was Peter Venezis, later awarded an OBE, and the forensic archaeologist was the world renowned Dr Sue Black. The pathologist told me that he had noticed a distinct pattern in the gunshot wounds found in the bodies he had been examining from Makoc and elsewhere. In very many cases, the fatal wound was a shot to the head from an AK47. The back of the skull was shattered, which indicated that the muzzle of the gun must have been placed against the head, as it was the gas discharged from the gun which entered the skull cavity and exploded the back of the head. A gunshot from a high powered rifle fired at a distance normally produces a small circular entry wound and a larger and more ragged exit wound with shards of bone facing in the direction of travel of the bullet. The skull would not be so extensively shattered as in these cases. Peter also noticed that the victims of this very close quarter shooting had received gunshot wounds in both sides of the chest, damaging both scapulae; there was also a shot to the groin. A couple of weeks after he had told me of his suspicions, I was on the site of an exhumation when I received a radio message from him to meet him in the mortuary room. I returned to the hospital and Peter showed me a corpse bearing the hall-marks of a shattered skull, gunshot wounds to chest and groin but also damage to the underside of the chin. Peter indicated to me a clear groove running up from the underside of the front of the chin into the brain cavity. That was it, the killers fired one shot into the left side of the victim's upper chest, then one to the opposite side, then a further shot into the groin to increase the pain and then the coup de grace with the muzzle under the chin and a single shot from the front so the victim could see his end coming. The gun shot pattern was of course, the sign of the cross.

The emotional strain was to become normal as exhumations continued over the next few weeks – a family of eight here, an old couple there, beaten and shoved face-down into a shallow pit. The nature of the people was a striking contrast with the wickedness which had been used against them. The victims and their families were by and large rural peasants, dressed poorly, quite often in old suits and waistcoats with discoloured shirts and often sporting berets in the French rural style of fifty years ago. I did start to notice that on a number of occasions, the Kosovo Albanians who had contacted ICTY investigators about murdered family members and who had been passed to us for action were young, in their mid-twenties and quite athletic. They would point out to us plots of land where their families had been buried, which was usually in and around the family home. I was later to find out that many of these young Kosovo Albanians were members of the UCK (Ushria Clirmtare e Kosoves), or KLA (Kosovo Liberation Army). The KLA had been classed by NATO as freedom fighters, but by Serbian authorities as terrorists. A pattern emerged of Kosovo Serbian police arriving at a house to arrest suspected UCK or KLA members only to find that they had fled the family home and were hiding in the mountains. The response was one very familiar in the Balkans; if they could not get the people they were after, they shot the parents and family instead. I was to see this again in Bosnia, where organised criminals threatened Bosnian police officers with threats of 'if you arrest us we will kill your children'; and they meant it.

The exhumation process involved military protection from the nationality in charge of that particular sector. Norwegian engineers deployed an armoured digger and I can swear that the Norwegian soldier driving it could peel a hard-boiled egg with the blade of the shovel. British bomb disposal soldiers (EOD) made a sweep of the site before we started our work and Royal Marines provided the lorry to transport the corpses back to the mortuary. They also pitched in and helped with the removal of bodies from the graves. It was awe-inspiring to watch soldiers from different nationalities welding together with the police in the difficult physical and emotional task of these recoveries. The disgust felt at the crimes committed and the sympathy for the families present was commonly experienced by us all and very tangible.

Quite incredibly, the identities of the killers were known to many eye witnesses. They were frequently local policemen or paramilitaries or often came from neighbouring villages. I was given a detailed list of one group of men from a Kosovan Serb village who had carried out a raid on a Muslim village not a mile away. They had killed their Muslim neighbours and taken away ploughs, horses and other livestock. I made sure to hand a statement we obtained to the ICTY investigators. Unfortunately, they told me that their threshold for prosecutions was only at the level of the commanders who organised the killings at the strategic and senior operational level. Crimes such as the ones I was reporting should be dealt with by the local police. Needless to say, no action was ever taken, partly because the old police service which was Serbian-dominated, had ceased to exist.

The policing of Kosovo after the NATO invasion was undertaken by the UN, using police officers from around the world. The country was still in chaos when I arrived. The infrastructure was dire; the roads were in atrocious condition and full of potholes. But amongst all this poverty one could not help noticing the large number of fairly new BMWs and Mercedes motor cars, not one of which bore licence plates! Many had been stolen from Western Europe and once they were driven back to Kosovo they disappeared into the unregulated chaos. There was little order and even less administration. The absence of regulation meant that almost anybody could drive a motor vehicle in almost any manner they felt like. The atrocious driving and lack of working traffic signals led the American UN police contingent to name two of the main intersections in Pristina as 'Suicide Corner' and 'Malfunction Junction' in police radio broadcasts and official reports.

After the autopsies of victims had been carried out at Pristina Hospital and in the event that no identification had been made, the victims' clothes were washed, dried photographed and handed on to the Organisation for Security and Co-operation in Europe (OSCE) who dealt with the identification thereafter. They would regularly hold 'clothes shows' in Pristina and surrounding towns. This involved recovered clothing being laid out in rows, frequently in old warehouses, where members of the local community were invited to attend and view the items. I visited several of these events and could feel the grief of those people hoping, or dreading, to catch sight of a familiar jacket or dress worn by a loved one who was still missing.

The officer in charge at the scenes of all the exhumations was a Hampshire inspector called Bob Lamburne. It was in Kosovo where I first met Bob, who I would meet again in Iraq. Bob was a well-nourished fellow with a heart as big as his frame, which was big. He was also a highly experienced crime scene investigator. At the end of every day we held a formal debrief where we would discuss the day's events. Problems would be highlighted, solutions discussed and I would outline the task for the next day, plus start times and special requirements. It was at one of these briefings that Bob told me that a nurse at Pristina hospital had come to the mortuary room and made a request. She was aware that we had exhumed the body of her brother and she asked Bob if she could see him. She explained that she had been working in Germany when the expulsions and killings of her people had taken place the year before and had not seen her brother since. She was aware that he had been killed and members of her family told her that his body had been exhumed by the British police. I was concerned about the state of the body and asked Bob as to its condition. He replied that it was a skeleton. No flesh, no form, just a bunch of white bones. What was I to say? I have had no training in such bereavement counselling and this was just a jumble of bones. 'No, Bob,' I said. 'Try and tell her there's nothing left, her brother has gone.'

The next day Bob came and found me again, 'It's no good, governor, she really wants to see the bones, there is no way I can dissuade her.'

'Ok, Bob' I said, exasperated. 'I will see her tomorrow afternoon when I visit the mortuary on my daily visit.'

The following day I met Bob and the nurse, who was called Flutura, at the hospital. She was an attractive woman, like most Kosovan women. She was a Muslim like her family and politely asked to see her brother's remains. She said that he was healthy and full of life when she left; she needed to see him now. I told her that he was no longer here; his spirit was with God, could she not remember him as he was and accept that all that was left behind were bones? She sobbed and sobbed and would not be moved; she wanted to see him. I could not help being upset by her crying and pitiful request. Okay, I thought, I have tried to shield you from the ugly truth, if you want to see a pile of bones then you can.

'Alright, alright,' I said. 'Be back here tomorrow at the same time in the afternoon and you can see him.' I left it with Bob to make the arrangements and have the remains formally lain out.

The next day, I attended the mortuary in the late afternoon. I met Flutura and Bob and then went into the mortuary alone. There, I met Steve Donlan a mortuary technician from Glasgow, whose day job was normally in the main hospital of that city. Steve had carefully laid out the skeleton on a stainless steel mortuary table so that all the bones were in exact order and resembled the familiar human shape. He had placed it on a single cotton sheet which Flutura had handed to Bob earlier. It was noticeable that on the left side of the skeleton, the arm and leg were shattered. I had come to notice that when people are being lined up to be shot they tend to face the left side of their body to the gunmen. Steve had clearly carried out a masterly job.

I called Flutura into the room. She approached the skeleton of her brother and cried. She sobbed as she picked up his skull and kissed it. She then wrapped the bones in the sheet of cotton upon which the bones lay in accordance with the Muslim tradition. She mumbled some words in Albanian, kissed my hand, thanked me profusely and left the room. Bob, Steve – witness of a thousand such encounters – and I were deeply and profoundly affected by Flutura. We all shed a tear that day.

Mick Clarke was another man like Bob. He was a constable with the South Yorkshire Police and was one of the permanent members of the team. He was one of the main diggers, a muscular man with miners as relatives and it showed. He had tremendous warmth with the villagers we met, who he organised to help us exhume their kin. He would also be sensitive enough to ensure that the next of kin got down into the trench with him and help carry the remains, which he would have put into a body bag, back to the army lorry. I also remember a somewhat amusing incident amongst all this mayhem. Once in the dead of night, I had occasion to go to the toilet in our accommodation block. I avoided putting the lights on as I did not want to wake anyone. I then reached in the dark for the toilet roll to find that the holder was empty. The nearest toilet was one floor down and I groaned, 'Oh, shit'. Just at that moment, I heard Mick's voice in the darkness and in his rich Yorkshire accent, 'Toilet roll, sir,' and from nowhere a toilet roll hovered in the darkness held in his thick hairy arms. 'We can't have you walking about like a crab can we, sir? Most unbecoming.' I couldn't help but to roar with laughter.

Not all the band were quite as easy to work with as Mick and Bob. I did experience a problem with one or two officers drinking too much of an evening and not making it out of bed for our early departure. This problem occurred soon after my arrival and was probably a way of testing how far the new boss could be pushed. We had been tasked with exhuming a family of eight from Orliane Podujevo, a village about five miles from the Serbian border and over an hour's drive away. I had arranged to meet the Royal Marines and bomb disposal troops at the site at 6am. We were all in our vehicles and ready to roll at 4.45am, except one of the team decided he wasn't ready and would come in his own good time; he couldn't give a damn and told me so. He was hung over and still drunk. I could see as clear as day he was testing my authority, he felt he had the experience, what does some country bumpkin from Dorset know? What I did know was that I was the boss and he would jump when I said so. I told him he had five minutes to be in the car or we were going without him. If he didn't make it he could spend the day arranging his return flight to England; I was fuming. Needless to say he made it. He then paid for his overconsumption of liquor by working harder than anyone else and we exhumed all eight victims. The corpses had been wrapped in plastic and were also below the water table. This had the effect of reducing the bodies to a human soup which created such a fetid stench that it was possible to smell the remains inside the lorry from 150 yards away. We then had to go to a nearby village and exhume the bodies of an elderly man and a woman who had been beaten to death by policemen from the Ministry of Interior. We even recovered the old man's walking stick. The Royal Marines performed sterling work that day; how they put up with the putrid smell for an hour and a half journey back to Pristina I do not know. I never had any more trouble from my miscreant friend again, though this kind of testing the new boss would recur again in later missions.

On a 'good day' we would manage ten exhumations, or sometimes just one or two depending on the location and circumstances. The mortuary team also worked with great industry and would get through six to eight autopsies a day. It takes on average at least three hours to carry out an autopsy on an average homicide (if there ever is such a thing) in the UK. In Kosovo, the mortuary team had to work much faster and their subjects had been dead a year. The corpses ranged from skeletons to decomposing bodies with a considerable amount of flesh remaining, depending on the soil type and moisture level in the location where they had been buried. In all but one of the cases we dealt with, death was due to multiple gunshot wounds, with AK47 bullets recovered from the bodies by the bucketful. In the majority of cases, the pathologist was able to prove that the killer was in close proximity to the victim when the fatal shots were fired, thus dispensing with any claims of accidental killing during a gun battle. This could have not been more evident when we exhumed the body of a Roma who had been used by the Serbs to bury some victims. He had been shot through the top of the head and the bullet was found to have tracked down through his body into his abdomen; he must have been on his knees begging for his life when he was killed. The scenes of the crimes were frequently burnt out villages or innocuous road sides where young men had been pulled out of a column of refugees and shot.

However, amongst all this bloodshed and murder, true humanity shone through. I usually had an interpreter with me, as it was vital to keep the local people fully informed about what we were doing and why. We also explained that the bodies would be returned to the communities after the autopsies had been completed, for reburial in their own (usually Muslim) tradition. I remember a group of villagers describing to me how the Serbs would ride around on their tanks and hold up a thumb and two fingers in a Serbian nationalist salute towards the villagers and shout, 'God fucks you.'

This form of three fingered salute has some Serb Christian Orthodox meaning and I said to my Muslim interpreter, 'These are not Christians.'

She said, 'I know that, I am your sister and you are my brother, so God is our father.' This lady, after all the injustice, cruelty and death she had seen shone with utter purity.

One of the last duties of my tour was the reburial of sixty-seven people who we had exhumed from in and around Makoc. The whole team pitched in and helped. The bodies were placed in coffins which had been delivered to the mortuary. Even Peter Venezis the world-renowned pathologist just rolled his sleeves up and carried bodies to the coffins. A convoy of lorries then took the deceased back to their village where, after speeches by the head-man and local dignitaries, the bodies were finally laid to rest.

After seven weeks of intensive long days, punctuated by only two days off, my secondment was finished – 135 bodies were recovered, the exhumation and evidential process was maintained and had run smoothly. The pattern of expulsions and systematic killing of Kosovo Albanians during early 1999 and the evidence gained by ICTY resulted in Slobodan Milosevic and his top four political aides being indicted for war crimes. Milosevic died in custody before adjudication.

I was driven to the airport in Skopje for my return flight home by one of my male interpreters. I can't remember why I said the following but I did. 'Yes, those bloody Serbs, they're all bastards.' I had been digging up their handiwork for the past seven weeks, what was I supposed to feel like?

He replied, 'No, Mr Nott, they are not all bad, I lived in Serbia before the war and they hid me. For weeks they hid me in their lofts and moved me to more Serb friends and more Serb friends until they got me across the border. My parents are still in Serbia and we have many friends there. The men who did this in Kosovo were criminals, nothing more.'

I learned a lot about the evil that men do in these seven weeks and I learned a lot about the dignity of the human spirit.

I returned home and was elated to see my wife again. I inhaled the beautiful pure air of Dorset and went back to work. There was a local furore ongoing at the time about the closure of the police house in Studland and the withdrawal of their village bobby. Studland has one of the most beautiful beaches in the country with white sand, chalk cliffs and a backdrop of rolling green hills. There is a quaint village nearby where everybody knows everybody but little in the way of crime. The chief constable welcomed me back to the force and then assigned me a task to produce a plan to enhance high visibility uniform police patrols and increase greater public reassurance in the police service. I felt that the perceived problems I had to deal with in Dorset paled somewhat into insignificance with what I had witnessed in the Balkans. I had caught the 'mission virus' as old hands say. There were bigger things going on in the world and I wanted a part in it.

Chapter Three
Bosnia

In December 2000, the Home Office was seeking to send eighty UK police officers to Bosnia to serve with the United Nations International Police Task Force (IPTF). The post of contingent commander was also advertised and set at the rank of superintendent. It seemed that the job was made for me. I talked about the posting, which would be for twelve months, with Judith. I thought that a year sounded like a long time and both Judith and I were unsure about spending that length of time apart, albeit there were generous periods of leave interspersed. I initially wrote an application for the job, then changed my mind and screwed it up and threw it in the bin. Judith and I talked about it again over Christmas and she felt that perhaps someone else may have been earmarked for the post and suggested I resubmit the application and 'just see what happens'. On my return from leave in early January 2001, I submitted the application and left it to fate. To my utter amazement, I was contacted by the Home Office in February and offered the position of contingent commander, to commence in October of that year.

On the 11 September 2001, I was working in my office in the Community Safety Department at the force headquarters in Winfrith, surrounded by fields of sheep. In the early afternoon, just after I had got back from a session in the gym, one of my colleagues, a retired sergeant said, 'Come and have a look at this guv, a plane has just crashed into a building in New York.' I went through to the press office which was just down the corridor and everyone was glued to the television screen. There were confused reports about a plane crashing into or near the Pentagon and the White House and there was all kinds of speculation about terrorism. It can't be; nobody would do that, I thought.

I have a vivid memory of the television pictures that clear sunny September day in New York. Then everyone in the room was astounded when we all saw the dreadful pictures live of a second aircraft ploughing into the second tower block alongside and exploding in a great ball of fire. We all watched stunned as the buildings burned, then collapsed in front of our eyes. I could not do or think of anything for a week; whilst I am not an American, I felt that our closest ally had been delivered a murderous wound to the heart of their country and the victims were just office workers and civilians, working to pay their mortgages, rent and grocery bills like the rest of us. The TV schedules were initially not altered but Judith and I channel-hopped continuously for news of the attacks until finally every British broadcaster on just about every channel covered the terrorist attacks continuously day after day. The world had changed forever.

On 3 October, after more tearful farewells with Judith, I drove to Stanstead Airport, where I met my Foreign Office contact and started to meet with the officers who comprised the next rotation. Forty officers were to fly out to replace the forty officers who had been in theatre for a year and who had completed their tour of duty. Amongst the new group was the man selected as my deputy, Chief Inspector Mick Ashton, a tall muscular Yorkshireman, a strong character with a quick wit and superb sense of humour. It was as well I had such a good deputy. Three officers had pulled out of the deployment in the last couple of weeks and a fourth had arrived at the hotel and promptly left again to return home. Despite a number of phone calls, she could not be persuaded to return. All four officers who had had second thoughts were female, I'm afraid to say. I think that separation from family and friends was the key issue. Our number had dropped already from forty to thirty-six.

We flew out the following morning and arrived in Sarajevo at around midday. The city bore considerable battle damage, with some buildings completely pockmarked with bullet and shell holes of various sizes. The area around the airport was devastated, with buildings reduced to shells. The tallest building in the city, a relatively modern office block which had formerly been occupied by the state broadcaster and television station, was in ruins. Sandbags were placed on the upper floors where the outside wall had been destroyed, leaving a skeleton-like structure. From these sand-bagged positions, snipers had terrorised the local civilian population as they had fetched and carried water and food. Sarajevo is a quite beautiful city and was an important urban centre for the Ottoman Empire in its push towards Western Europe. It later came within the sphere of the Austro-Hungarian Empire and benefitted from Austrian architecture with more than a hint of the 'Near East'. Many buildings, particularly those in the 'old city', had masonry ground floors crowned by overhanging ornately carved wooden upper floors traditionally Ottoman in style. The diverse architectural styles were complemented by Mosques and churches, both Catholic and Orthodox. Bosnia and Herzegovina, to give it its full title, is made up of Croats, Serbs and Bosniaks (Bosnian Muslims). The greater part of Bosnia was captured by the Ottomans in the Middle Ages but the Krajina region of Croatia resisted the Ottoman invasion. Washed up here by the tide of history were Serbs who fought the Ottomans and remained in an enclave inside Croatia. It was here that the high water mark of the Ottoman Empire reached its zenith and as it receded it left behind communities of Serbs and Muslims. Tito did his best to blend all these peoples together, all South Slavs, (Yugoslavia literally means South Slavs) but ultimately failed.

The incoming rotation of thirty-six UK officers underwent training with the UN from the history of the Balkans and current political dynamics and personalities, down to UN administration and how to refuel your vehicle. I was also involved with Mick

Ashton every evening in working with officers and UN personnel to ensure that those with particular skill sets were utilised to the best advantage of the mission and to replace the outgoing forty officers. At the end of the week, the thirty-six officers were deployed all around Bosnia to individual IPTF Police Stations. From these IPTF stations, the international police would monitor and help train the local police in the areas in which they were situated. This monitoring and training extended to all ranks, from the patrol policeman and woman up to the senior officers in their respective areas. Mick Ashton went north to Banja Luka; I was to remain in Sarajevo.

Bosnia and Herzegovina (BiH) has a small coastline on the Adriatic and is to the east of Italy and Austria, the west of Turkey and Greece and south of Hungary. It has a population of four million of which forty-four per cent are Bosniaks, thirty-one per cent Serb and seventeen per cent Croat. The remainder are made up of seventeen different ethnic groups, the majority of which are Roma. The men are all about six foot six inches tall and of muscular build; the women are not much less than six-foot-tall, of slim build, with high cheek bones, dark hair and slanted, almond-shaped brown eyes. Politically, the country was divided into three segments; the Federation of Bosnia and Herzegovina, made up of ten cantons populated mainly but not wholly by Croats and Bosniaks; the Republika Srbska (RS), misleadingly named to give the initial impression of being a separate country, mirrors the Federation; and the District of Brcko, which is a small canton in the North. The local police were stationed in the ten cantons and answered to the Ministry of Interior (MOI) in Sarajevo; the Police in the RS were stationed in public security centres and answered to their own MOI in Banja Luka and the District of Brcko ran themselves. The IPTF under the UN and in cooperation with the government of BiH were building a state border service to secure their borders and a state police to be called the State Investigation and Protection Agency (SIPA) but were not yet formed.

The mission of the IPTF was to contribute to the establishment of the rule of law by assisting in reforming and restructuring the local police, assessing the function of the existing judicial system and monitoring and auditing the performance of the police. This was achieved by monitoring, advising and supporting the local police at police station and headquarters level and a substantial amount of support was given to training and minority recruitment. Another important function was monitoring the process of the return of former refugees to their original homes from which they had been evicted or forced to flee. It has been estimated that over 2.2 million people were displaced by the civil war. The IPTF comprised 1,795 police personnel from 44 different countries.

During my first week in the mission and during the training phase, I was called to see the IPTF Commissioner, Brigadier General Vincent Coeurderoy, of the French gendarmerie. He was an utter gentleman of the highest integrity and professional ability; he told me that I was to be posted to Sarajevo to work as the deputy to Gordon Black, a superintendent with the Royal Canadian Mounted Police. The unit to which I was assigned was called the Joint Task Force and dealt with high profile cases and terrorist related crime. I found Gordon to be a very upright, confident and competent police officer, fiercely and proudly Canadian. The unit was engaged in monitoring and supporting a number of serious cases including the investigation into the murder of Jozo Leutar, the Federal Minister of Interior, who was killed by a bomb explosion in 1999. He had been working hard on the integration of Muslim police officers into the Federation police before he was murdered. The murder investigation had originally been conducted by senior Federal Ministry of Interior officers but the investigation was considered to be unsatisfactory. It seems that they had originally suspected Muslim extremists, but missed the obvious that the killers were Croat nationalists angry at Mr Leutar's inclusive policies. Other crimes which I would be later involved in monitoring and assisting with were the murders of several Croat police officers and Croat civilians in Travnik central Bosnia, a mixed Croat and Muslim area. In my first week on the unit, I was assigned a Croatian lady to be my interpreter. Her name was Jasna Peric; she defined herself as

Croatian but had a Serbian stepfather and her grandmother had been an advisor to the King of Serbia before the Second World War. She was a widow in her fifties and had lived in Sarajevo during the siege of the city, in which her main task was to carry large water containers to her family, which she filled from the river Miljacka running through the centre of Sarajevo. Jasna was an elegant and sophisticated lady who I would describe as a Bosnian aristocrat in reduced circumstances. On top of her considerable skills in English, her integrity and firm character, she knew just about every senior police officer and prosecutor in the country.

My first assignment was to review the murders of the Croat police officers in Travnik. The brief facts were that several Croat civilians were killed in their houses between August and October 1997. Three of those who were killed and two of the wounded were all returnees to Travnik, having been forced to leave during the civil war. They were all deliberately targeted; one was killed by a claymore anti-personnel mine and the others were shot in separate attacks. In addition to this, three Croat police officers were killed and one wounded in and around the police station in Travnik when going to or coming off duty. They were killed in three separate bomb explosions. I spent some time gathering all the paperwork and then set off with Jasna to meet the head of CID for the Federation at the Ministry of Interior in central Sarajevo. I wished to make a start by meeting the police officer now in overall charge of these murders, but as a matter of protocol wanted to first go to the most senior officer, Dragan Lukac. We arrived in good time but were kept waiting outside his office for some considerable period. We were eventually led into his plush suite, which was well furnished with leather sofas, chairs and assorted plants. Sitting behind a grand desk, I saw the inhabitant, Mr. Dragan Lukac. He was immaculately dressed in a dark suit and waistcoat; he was a large-framed man of about six foot six inches tall, aged in his mid- forties and with an unsmiling angular face with a grimace which could turn a pint of milk sour.

Without any attempt at a welcome or pleasantries – he would have known something about me from Jasna when she booked the appointment – he said, barely glancing up at me, 'What do you want? My time is very valuable.'

I explained that I had been asked by Brigadier General Coeurderoy of the IPTF to review the case of the Travnik murders and that I would like to go there and speak to his police who were involved in the investigations.

He replied in a firm and aggressive manner that it was solely a matter for the Minister of Interior.

I reminded him that the investigation of major crime was a police matter and that I was well within the UN mandate. I also reminded him that in any event, the Minister was very happy for the UN IPTF to review the case as he and Brigadier General Coeurderoy were in agreement about the subject.

He said, 'Whatever the MOI instructs, I will do.'

I gave him a jaunty nod of the head, thanked him for his valuable time and left without further ado. Our relationship was business-like from then on. At the end of the day, I had to remember that it was his country and he probably resented the interference from outsiders, necessary as it was. I noticed that all the doors to the offices of the Minister and the chiefs of police in the building were double doors, separated from each other by about three inches. Obviously no one trusted anyone!

Having cleared the way with the Chief, I then drove with Jasna to Travnik, which is about an hour and a half drive from Sarajevo. I visited the scenes of the crimes of these murders in order to feel my way into the case. The detective is always looking for similarities, patterns and the atmosphere of the scene. I met with the local police at Travnik police station, a place around which several murders had occurred. This is where I first came across Anto Simic, the head of CID for the Federal Ministry of Interior, which broadly means he represented all ten cantons. He was a Croatian by ethnicity and I can only describe him as a warm, sincere gentleman in his mid-fifties with a wealth of experience. We discussed the murders and he said that he had only been assigned these cases recently and had not been the original investigating officer. The more I dug into the cases, it became increasingly clear that the initial investigations had been very badly handled and the original investigation team had wrongly assumed that the killers were Croat nationalists as in the Leutar killing.

Jasna also took me to see Marinko Durcevic, the Chief Prosecutor for the Federation of BiH. He was a gentleman of quiet disposition, whose life and indeed the lives of his family were under threat from Islamic extremists. The types of people subject to his investigations were killers who would have had no compunction but to execute him if ever they got the chance. He had already been involved in some successful prosecutions of Islamic terrorists. As a result of my meeting with him and after assessing the threats against him to be very real, I went to see the Minister of Interior for the Federation who agreed to provide armed protection for Mr Durcevic. One thing I had overlooked when I arrived in Bosnia was the legal system. In England and Wales, the USA, Canada, Australia, New Zealand and some other Commonwealth countries the criminal law is based on the common law which has developed over time immemorial. Under our common law system, the police are the lead criminal investigation agency. This follows through into an adversarial system in court where the prosecution have to prove the case, with the defence testing the evidence and putting forward their own arguments. Bosnia, like many other European countries use the Civil Law or Napoleonic system, where crime investigation is led by the prosecutor with the police acting under his or her direction. Whilst in the civil law system the police are able to question suspects, it is the questioning by prosecutors which carries the weight. The initial court hearings involve an inquisitorial process by the prosecutor, examining magistrate or judge, which puts the court in the lead in the investigation process. Therefore, when engaged on police reform, monitors from 'common law' countries must grasp this fact early on, as must military forces who sometimes expect the local police to be like their own countrymen in the UK or USA and entirely forget the vital role of the prosecutor. The relationship I was fortunate to have formed with Mr Durcevic so soon after my arrival, would prove crucial to my later work in BiH.

I assigned two British police officers to the Travnik murders permanently. Their first job was to obtain copies of all papers relating to the investigation and get it all translated. Within a few days, they had collected a room full of papers, all of which were in the local language and would take months to translate. It became clear as we read through the early investigation reports that the initial police enquiries were inefficiently conducted and lacked the rigour and flair of the more intuitive detective.

As time drew on, the British officers uncovered a line of enquiry which had hitherto been surprisingly ignored by the local police. This involved a group of Mujahedeen who had come to Bosnia to fight for the Muslims. The British officers directed and assisted the local police in the renewed investigation, which resulted in the uncovering of a major Al-Qaida terrorist living in Bosnia. This individual was wanted in Italy for a major terrorist crime but no extradition treaty existed between Bosnia and Italy. Certain Italian Carabinieri I worked with proposed to arrange his abduction and to fly him by helicopter back to Italy. This seemed a good idea to me, which is probably why I never became a chief constable. I raised the prospect of this practical solution with the general but he was not keen.

'The rule of law must operate in Bosnia,' he quite rightly stated.

Arrangements were then put in hand to strip this individual of his Bosnian citizenship, which he had gained by marrying a local girl. If his citizenship was removed, he could then be legitimately deported; his country of origin was in North Africa but one which had warm relations with Italy. The flight could have involved a stop in a country with an extradition treaty with Italy and he could have been arrested as he was changing planes or as he sat on the initial outbound aircraft. An application was made to the courts to strip the suspect of his citizenship, whilst simultaneously he was put under surveillance by the local police. The surveillance team followed him around Travnik and he was seen to enter the local mosque. Observations were maintained for several hours but he was not seen to emerge. It then dawned on the local policemen watching him that a lone woman in a burka who came out of the mosque was the only person they had seen there all day. In a panic, they contacted their senior officers who authorised an immediate raid on the mosque, but they were too late; he had escaped dressed as a woman. This terrorist and the major suspect for the Travnik killings had escaped and despite a country wide search has never been seen since. He is currently (2016) one of the most wanted Al-Qaida terrorists on international alert lists in the world. For sound investigative reasons I do not wish to reveal his name, nor the crime he was wanted for in Italy.

My initial baptism in working with and for the UN rushed in upon me within the first weeks of my arrival. Whilst struggling with how to operate the washing machine in my apartment and learning how to negotiate the purchase of a loaf of bread and other basic lifesaving domestic arrangements, I was visited in my office on the upper floor of the UN office block by Janet Grobbalar, an IPTF monitor from South Dakota, USA. She was a US police officer on secondment who displayed a serious and sombre countenance. I don't think I ever saw her smile or display any kind of emotion.

'Doctor Gravel wants to see you,' she said in a monotone voice.

'Who's he?' I said.

'A political advisor on floor two, he wants you to see him now,' she replied.

This sounded like a royal command. I got up and went down stairs and entered his rather spartan office. Janet walked in and announced me. Dr Bob Gravel was a slight man in his mid-forties with an angry face. Without further introductions, this is how it went.

'OK, Nott, [pronounced Natt in his Canadian accent] I want an operation order by next Tuesday [it was Wednesday today] for the police throughout the whole of BiH. I want them stopping cars, checking out folk, seizing guns and ammunition and I want the police in Croatia and Serbia to copy the plan and do it themselves, any questions?'

'I can't put something like that together in that sort of time, I need to consult, assess and travel to the different regions to do it, I need ...' and before I could finish the sentence, he said, 'Do you want this job or not? I can find somebody else to do it, they told me you were the best guy for the job.'

I said, 'Okay, I can do it but I need more time.'

'Okay,' he said. 'You got to Wednesday.'

I left his office in a daze; this was not how policing worked. I was used to putting this kind of operation together in Dorset, but I would take a month, consulting with commanders, obtaining the staff, preparing intelligence packages and so on, but a week throughout the whole country of disparate players? But I had to do it, I was on test and this was a whole different world to Dorset.

I returned to my office and saw Gordon Black. I told him what had happened, 'Oh, Tony, sorry; I forgot to tell you. Are you okay with it?'

'Looks like I've got to be,' I said. 'Who's this Bob Gravel?'

Gordon told me he was a Canadian who was very influential in the mission, what he wants has to be got done. 'He's quite mad, of course,' he added.

Well, I had no time to lose. I could see what was needed. I had to create an operation in which the Serb, Croat and Bosniak elements in the local police would work together. I could bring in the newly formed State Border Service and focus on increased stop and searches of vehicles. The criminal intelligence units within the local police, (which also had IPTF members working in them) could trawl through their data bases and throw up all suspected drug dealers and handlers of stolen goods. If the Prosecutor was okay, we could launch the operation with a series of dawn raids. All I had to do was sell it to the locals.

Thanks to Jasna's charm and influence with the local police, she managed to get the Chief of CID for the Federation, RS, Brcko and State Border Service into the UN building the next day. I told Janet to tell Dr Gravel what I was doing and he sent a message back to me that he would address them at the start of my meeting. This he duly did in his blunt, no nonsense, North American way. He told them what he wanted; an operation order by Tuesday, no ifs, no buts, no delays, no prevarication, just get it done. Without a by-your-leave, he turned on his heel and walked out of the room. For the second time in two days I was stunned; he had wild eyes, a menacing tone and a total lack of empathy with those he was addressing. I then got down to the business of injecting some humanity into the occasion. Whilst in full uniform, I explained that I was a CID man like themselves and was in the same boat as they were and we all needed to come up with a plan. Amongst the senior detectives in the room was Anto Simic, the head of CID who I had met in Travnik. We discussed our task and all expressed a willingness to put an operation together. Communication between the different parts of Bosnia had been awkward due to the civil war and I could see that the men in this room, despite their war-time differences, still wanted to fight crime and criminals which caused misery to all of the local people regardless of ethnicity. They agreed to task their criminal intelligence departments to come up with a list of people in respect of whom they could obtain search warrants. I told them I would come up with some kind of matrix to record statistics which they could all access and I would design a common stop and search form which their patrol officers could use with guidance notes. They were okay with that; the fact that I had six months earlier written the Dorset Police stop and search policy was helpful. The meeting ended surprisingly optimistically, despite the Gravel factor. I also set up a co-ordination office in the UN headquarters and they were all happy to send their arrest details, drugs and weapon seizures to this single point. I had already worked out a centralised system whereby I would have all the arrest details of criminals from across the country recorded in one place, which I would then share with them on a monthly basis. Therefore, I was able to destroy any notion of secrecy and all Bosnian police forces would receive the same criminal intelligence. The operation, rightly or wrongly, would display to each law enforcement agency what they and their neighbours were doing and introduce an element of competition which is a good motivator to do more.

Under Marshal Tito, the defence of Yugoslavia had been designed around a local protection concept. Every village and town had a quartermaster who stored arms and ammunition for the local resistance force. Had Yugoslavia been invaded by NATO (or indeed Soviet Russia) during the Cold War, the local resistance forces would have taken to the forests and mountains and embarked on a guerrilla war, making it impossible for NATO to capture; just like Tito had prevented the Nazis from ever subduing the country in the Second World War.

NATO, and in particular the British army, did an outstanding job during the period after 1995 when SFOR[1] was established. British soldiers recovered hundreds of tons of guns, bombs, mines and other articles of war from the towns and villages. The military were keen to devolve this role to the local police, who were ultimately responsible in peace time for upholding the law. I saw the timely opportunity which the military thinking presented and increased focus on the seizure of weapons. I named the operation 'Common Purpose', which the local police also liked the sound of and it commenced on schedule on the Wednesday following as planned. After some initial successes and the odd glitch, I went on holiday at Christmas leaving the operation in the hands of a British officer; there wasn't much to do other than collect the statistics at the end of the month and circulate them to all those involved. However, mischief was afoot. When I was back home on leave, I had a dream one night before Christmas in which I had just got into bed and put my legs down to the bottom of the bed under the duvet when they touched something, I threw the cover back to see a snake slithering towards me. I woke up in a start and blind panic. I told my wife about it and she said, 'It's a snake in the bed, there is someone close to you and they don't like you!' I put it out of my mind, like I do when I don't always want to hear something bad. However, upon my return to Sarajevo from leave, I was greeted by a rather exuberant senior IPTF officer who told me that 'Operation Common Purpose' had been suspended. The cause was the failure of the local police to provide the monthly statistics and apparently there was also a lack of secure fax machines. I got hold of Jasna and had her phone every senior local policeman involved in the operation and discovered that the difficulties were not of their making.

The main cause of the problem was a lazy British IPTF monitor who saw the task I had given him as being a bit of an inconvenience to his social life and aggravated by an overly ambitious (North American) senior officer who didn't want me to outshine him. After a heated discussion with the individuals concerned and some frantic phone calls to my Bosnian counterparts, fully aided by Jasna, the operation jumped back into life and ran for the full six months as was intended. Jasna whispered in my ear that while I had been away on leave, the senior officer and the constable had been sharpening knives to put in my back. Fortunately, with good intelligence coming from Jasna (and another person in the office), I was able to stay one step ahead in this snake pit in which I now found myself. Despite the internal office politics, the operation proved to be an overwhelming success, much to the disappointment of my foreign rival and I made a positive impact personally causing him increased resentment. Literally tons of arms and thousands of rounds of ammunition were recovered by the local police, in addition to stolen property and contraband.

For me, the greatest success was the inadvertent formation of a group of senior CID officers from all over the country who met together to discuss the operation and the new investigative opportunities which presented themselves. I initially chaired the group which was eventually joined by the recently promoted state prosecutor (none other than Mr Durcevic) and we met in different parts of the country each month. The effect was to bond all these officers together and we met monthly for the next two years to discuss and plan 'cross border crime' and police operations. As a bonus, each police force area also got involved in trying to out-do each other in the hospitality stakes and I sadly became used to Bosnian mixed meat platters served on a plate the size of a dustbin lid, followed by a sweet course of pastry covered in treacle and semi liquid sugar overlaid with almonds. A very Ottoman throwback. Needless to say the whole thing was washed down with Rakia or Slivovitz, the local brandy or, more accurately, fire water.

Chapter Four
The Case of the Red Mercury

Brigadier General Coeurderoy was a perfect and gallant French gentleman. However, working for him was a French major of gendarmerie, Niccolo Le Gaul, who had something of the night about him. He introduced himself to me as a special advisor to the general and added, 'For whom I would gladly die.' He was convinced that Gordon Black and the Joint Task Force were failing to keep him aware of sensitive criminal terrorist matters and he threatened that if he found out that he was not being informed of important matters, then serious action would be taken. 'There must be no secrets between us,' he firmly stated. What he actually meant was that there were to be no secrets held back from him, but what he chose to tell us was another matter.

In mid-November, just over a month after my arrival, Louis Philippe (LP) a French lieutenant of gendarmes entered my office and told me that a senior Bosnian police officer at Interpol in Sarajevo had received some information about cigarette smuggling and wished to see me about it. In a country that had seen murder on an industrial scale, I couldn't get that excited about a lorry load of smuggled cigarettes, but there was something in how LP related the story that made me agree to visit his counterpart in Interpol. I took with me a fellow UK police constable, Mick Carpon, who also worked on the Joint Task Force.

As we drove along Kolodvorska Street towards the Interpol office, LP said, 'What do you know about red mercury?'

'Nothing,' I said. 'I've never heard of the stuff.'

'Nor do I,' he replied. He looked away and would not look me in the eyes again; something told me that he knew a lot more than what he was telling me.

When we arrived at the Interpol office, I met with the officer in command, Boris Manic, who said to LP, 'He's not here yet, can Mr Nott wait?'

'Okay, LP, what's going on, this is about more than a lorry load of cigarettes?'

'Oui, yes' he said. 'We have a man who has information about a large amount of red mercury which can be made into a nuclear bomb.'

Boris added through an interpreter, 'Yes, it has all been stolen from Russia following the collapse of the Soviet Union; it could fall into the hands of terrorists.'

I said, 'Who are we waiting for?'

Boris explained that he had a friend who worked in the State Border Service (SBS) who was running an informant and he wished to tell us about the red mercury. Apparently, the SBS officer didn't trust any of his own senior officers. Mick Carpon told me, out of earshot of Boris, that many Bosnian police were corrupt and it sounded like we had a major terrorist job in action. I wasn't so sure.

Eventually, the officer from the State Border Service arrived and I spent the next two hours trying to unravel his story. The brief synopsis was that he had established a link into a gang of smugglers, whose usual business involved the transport of counterfeit cigarettes, made elsewhere in Eastern Europe, then smuggled into Bosnia where they were sold at the market price of the brand they mimicked. His informant, an active cigarette smuggler, had met a Russian criminal who told him he had in his possession 30kg of red mercury, which he said was of weapons grade and had come from a Russian ship yard. The Russian travelled between Vienna and Slovenia but the cigarette smuggler didn't know where the Russian was living. He said the Russian was willing to sell the red mercury for $50,000. The SBS officer suggested that if the UN could come up with the money, then he could arrange through his informant to buy the mercury and avoid a terrorist attack of unimaginable proportions. LP and Mick Carpon's eyes were like saucers as the tale unfolded. I asked the SBS officer why he had not told his own senior officers about this information and he insisted that they were corrupt and in league with the smugglers. I had met some senior SBS officers during the planning of Operation Common Purpose and thought they appeared to me to be an honest bunch. You get feelings about people and my feelings about this individual were not so positive. He only knew his informant by the name of Miladin the Slovene and he had no idea of the Russian's name, where he came from, or how he had got hold of this material. I asked him if he could fix up a meeting between the informant and me, to which he agreed. I kept open the possibility of the UN coming up with $50,000 as I wanted to keep the job running. I didn't tell LP of my reservations but Mick Carpon was convinced by the story. I later heard that he and LP had discussed the case with enthusiasm and were not impressed with what they saw as my lacklustre approach.

When I got back to the office I made some checks regarding red mercury. The Russian newspaper *Pravda* ran a story in 1993, which claimed that red mercury was a super-conductive material used for producing high-precision conventional and nuclear bombs. The paper claimed to have had access to leaked top secret Kremlin reports. I also checked with some military friends I had made in SFOR, who were more sceptical about such a substance and doubted it even existed at all.

Over the next few days there was complete silence from Interpol and the SBS officer and I waited in vain for my appointment with the link man Miladin the Slovene and the Russian entrepreneur. I repeatedly asked LP to chase up our helpful SBS officer and he told me he was doing his best, but I noticed he had a sheepish manner when he spoke. What I didn't know was that the French were busy themselves and a certain major of gendarmes wanted to grab some glory by seizing the terrorists' cookbook ingredients of the century. One evening about a week later, I was phoned in my apartment at ten o'clock.

Gordon Black told me that Major Le Gaul had personally led a troop of federal Ministry of Interior police, accompanied by an all-French UN IPTF team of monitors and arrested four persons in possession of red – and indeed grey – mercury. It appeared to be the arrest of the epoch, with terrorists arrested in Sarajevo complete with weapons grade red and grey mercury. I was hopping mad when Gordon told me about this operation; this was my job, I was on the case, how did they get involved and why had we in the Joint Task Force been cut out? I was furious and was going to take this straight to the top. A serious attempt had been made to stab me in the back and derail operation Common Purpose, now I was going to be made to look inept over my failure to recover this nuclear material. Furthermore, what had actually happened and what had actually been recovered?

The next morning all became clear. I steamed into the general's office brushing past his Chief of Staff and into the inner office where I saw the general and a rather subdued Major Le Gaul.

'I see you made some arrests, major. How come I wasn't told?'

Unusually, the general lacked his normal self-confidence and presence. He turned to me and said, 'It was late, Tony and we didn't want to disturb you. But it's nothing anyway, the substance was made from sawdust or something similar, it was just an attempt to trick money out of the UN.' The matter had clearly been an embarrassment.

I thanked the general, threw a look at Le Gaul which could have been taken for a sly smile, saluted the general and left. Policing, nor indeed human nature doesn't change anywhere in the world you work, there will always be some bugger trying to steal the glory. Red Mercury was later found to be a substance of dubious if not mythical origin.[2]

Chapter Five
Banja Luka

In mid-February 2002, Brigadier General Coeurderoy appointed me to the post of regional commander for the UN region of Banja Luka in the north of the country and within the ethnically Serb part of the country called the Republika Srbska (RS). I had a staff of 250 IPTF monitors, including my deputy Major Robert Zolkiewski, a Polish officer of aristocratic heritage and impeccable manners; a Ukrainian Chief of Personnel, Volodomyr Leychenko, who looked like Trotsky with his round spectacles; and a Russian political advisor, Fyodor (Theodore) Klimchyk, who possessed a sharp brain and a deep and unambiguous understanding of the region and its people. I had only a few days to move, packed up my meagre possessions from my apartment in Sarajevo into a metal trunk and travelled after work on a dark evening in a blizzard to my new home, a flat above a shop in a side street off the main thoroughfare of Banja Luka. The journey took nearly five hours and I could only just make out the road as I drove over the mountains and through forests. The snow was coming down like stair rods the like of which I had never seen before. I had thought about travelling the next morning but was afraid of being thought of as a softie by my eastern European colleagues who see this type of blizzard as just a shower.

Banja Luka is a city of 250,000 people and the capital of the RS. It was captured by the Ottoman Turks during the expansion of that empire in the Middle Ages and the Hadija grand mosque was built there in 1580. It was by all accounts a spectacular religious building but completely destroyed by Serb nationalists during the civil war of 1991 to 1995. Attempts to rebuild it were challenging in the extreme and it was only completed in 2016. Banja Luka is surrounded by mountains and forests and the southern approach into the city follows the river Vrbas which, like all Bosnian rivers, is deep green in colour and cuts through a spectacular gorge nicknamed 'Cheddar Gorge' by NATO and the British army in particular who occupied this northern sector. In the centre of the town is a square surrounded by a dozen or more busts on plinths of resistance fighters, both men and women who died or were executed fighting the Nazis. Each bust has garlands of flowers around the neck. Banja Luka was a central point around which fierce resistance to the Nazis was made. It became so problematic that an area outside the city was ringed by German troops and all those within the ring were killed. To add to this ocean of blood, a small village outside of the city was attacked by Croatian Nazi sympathisers and all the inhabitants, men women and children had their throats cut. Croatian fascists occupied the city and the Ustase, as they were called, deported thousands of Serbs and destroyed Orthodox churches. These atrocities have not been forgotten and formed part of the seeds of civil war.

The major problem facing the UN IPTF in Banja Luka was the supervision of the return of refugees to their homes who had fled during the 1991-5 civil war. The majority of these people were Muslims, with a smaller number of Croats. After people had left or been forced out of their houses, they were taken over by Bosnian Serbs, similar to the Nazis occupying houses vacated by Jews in the Sudetenland. Whilst the number of people returning to their homes was encouraging, deeper analysis revealed that the incumbents in the houses they had occupied would strike deals with the true owners and in effect buy the house for what amounted to a knock down price. Many of the returnees did not want to stay in areas where they felt unsafe and where so many bitter memories would haunt them. By the time I arrived in

Bosnia, the UN had helped over 600,000 out of a total of over 2 million people return to their homes.

Crime in Banja Luka was not dissimilar to that in the UK and on the whole, offences involving dishonesty were far fewer. However, due to the existence of so many firearms, violent crime tended to be more serious than at home. On one occasion, a drunken man wandered onto the runway at Banja Luka airport throwing hand grenades around. The local police responded to what would have been a national emergency in the UK and concluded their report with the words 'man taken home drunk and handed over to wife, bucket full of hand grenades confiscated!' On another occasion, a farmer, who had been experiencing problems with sheep from a neighbouring farm wandering onto his land and eating all his animal feed, tried to solve the problem by laying a chain of anti-personnel mines along his boundary. He blew up several sheep before the local police intervened and advised against this practice.

Another problem I had as a UN IPTF commander was the appalling standard of driving by some of the IPTF monitors. Some of the driving standards of participating nations were even worse. On one occasion, I was called out from my office to Cheddar Gorge where beneath the emerald green surface of the river Vrbas I could see a white UN vehicle lying on its side. It had plunged about a hundred feet off the road down the ravine and into the river. Fortunately, our relationship with the British army was excellent and being British myself added to the advantage. I managed to wheedle around a major in the Royal Engineers who sent a crane; our UN vehicle was hauled out of the river much to the amusement of the locals who made great merriment at our catastrophe. Luckily it was only our pride that was damaged.

The driver and passenger were both Bangladeshi police officers. Bapu the driver later told me that he had swerved off the road as a local car was being driven straight at him. There were no crash barriers and his vehicle went between two boulders and 'jumped down' (his words) into the river. By some incredible stroke of luck, they were both thrown clear before the vehicle disappeared into the river. I had already seen too many reports about bad driving by UN personnel. I was determined to make my mark on this problem and was going to roast Bapu alive for endangering himself and his colleague plus writing off a UN vehicle. When he was wheeled into my office later that day and I guess noticing my stern countenance, he all but kneeled down in front of me with his hands clasped together, one of them bandaged. I told him it was only by the mercy of God that he and his colleague, Abdul, were still alive. He clasped his hands and prayed looking skyward and handed me his UN driving licence and said he didn't want to drive any more. I gladly took it from him as was my intention and sent him away relieved that he had to face no more punishment. I visited his friend Abdul in hospital where he had been kept for a check-up; he laid to attention and saluted from his bed. He seemed very happy, but a little embarrassed at being visited by a senior officer, which he had not expected; he was discharged a couple of hours later. From then on, I sent out a memo to all my station commanders that, should a UN vehicle be involved in any accident where only one vehicle was involved and no witnesses were to hand, then the driver was to be immediately suspended from driving for the duration of their tour. All monitors in my region were to be given a copy of my memo. I am glad to say that after that, the number of accidents involving UN vehicles rapidly dropped and I did feel pleased in my new role as a martinet.

In the summer of that year, Judith came out to stay with me in my apartment for a month or so. I must say it was lovely to have her company on a regular basis again as mission life can be lonely. Now, the Bosnian Serbs in Banja Luka were not generally too fond of the British, somewhat on account of the RAF bombing them in 1995. Judith met with some coldness when she set out to do the shopping but is herself a feisty lady and chief flower arranger at her church. She is not a shrinking violet and unlikely to be easily intimidated. She plonked herself in shops and stood her ground when confronted with some hostility and I think generally won over all those she came into contact with. She became very friendly with several local women, including my secretary, Dushanka, another Balkan lady with the cut of Jasna.

Dushanka was of Serbian heritage, a sensitive lady with a strong sense of justice. She discussed the miners' strike at length with Judith and was upset at the handling of it by the UK police and government. I have found that many people who lived under Communism, (including policemen from the former East Germany) have retained a deep social conscience.

On Friday 19 July 2002, I had the usual busy day in the office but one problem was bubbling. At the extreme north of Bosnia in the Republika Srbska and within the area of Prijedor was the village of Kostajnicia, which borders Croatia. This was the border over which certain politicians within the RS wanted to make mischief. Kostajnicia is a small town situated just south of the river Una on the northern border of Bosnia and Herzegovina within the Bosnian Serb region of the RS. On the opposite side of the river is Hrvatska Kostajnicia, which from the end of the civil war in 1995 became a part of Croatia. The two small towns are separated by a bridge over the river. To complicate matters, a small medieval stone fortress is on the southern bank but, surrounded by a ditch, is almost an island. This castle was regarded as a Croat defence against the Ottomans and when Yugoslavia was divided up at the end of the civil war the castle was considered by the politicians and international community to be within Croatia and the border placed at the southern end of the bridge and just south of the castle. However, due to disputes between the politicians in Bosnia and Croatia, the bridge had remained closed since the end of the war. As Kostajnicia and Hrvatska Kostajnicia were in effect the same town cut in half by a river, families were divided by this impasse and they were forced to make a twenty-mile round trip to visit their relations and friends. It was election year for local politicians in the RS and the mayor wanted to be re-elected. Nothing was going to inspire Bosnian Serbs more than strong nationalist rhetoric about the strength and unity of the Serbs and how in this case they were going to take back the castle and extend the internationally agreed border to the centre of the river.

UN diplomatic officials had been in communication with politicians from the RS that Friday as it had been rumoured that an attempt was being made by RS authorities to extend the border by about 100m northward. I became aware of this growing tension during the day, but preferred to leave the matter in the hands of the politicians and wanted no UN uniform presence there as I did not want to get sucked into a toxic mix of political scheming.

At about nine o clock that evening, the phone went in my apartment; it was Bob Gravel. 'Tony, you got to get down to the border at Kostajnicia. The mayor is pushing the border of BiH one hundred metres into Croatia. He's forcing an international incident; if that border stays, the Croats will send armed police to push it back. I can't get up there, I'm five hours away and committed with another problem. Keep me informed.' Then before he hung up, he added, 'Oh, and by the way, some Croat politicians are putting pressure on SFOR to intervene, which could mean armed NATO soldiers on the streets in Kostajnicia and likely to exacerbate things even more.'

With a bad feeling in my stomach, I realised that I had been given the mother of all peace-keeping operations and had to act fast. Fortunately, the British army are very professional at establishing local contacts 'in theatre'. I was one of those local contacts and I got straight on the phone to Chris Powell a New Zealand major serving with the British army at an old steel works known as 'the Metal Factory', their base in Banja Luka. Chris and I had frequently had dinner together in their mess and we had forged a good working relationship. I outlined the issue to him, but before I finished speaking he told me that General Van Diepenbrugge had already dispatched a platoon of soldiers. I asked him to hold back and let me try to resolve this first with no army in sight; if I needed him, I would shout. I had a UN radio which had the military channel, so I could communicate direct. He agreed with my request, making sure that was what I wanted. As a beat policeman dealing with a bunch of hooligans, the last thing I ever did was to approach an unruly group in a macho, 'I'm a bigger man than you', type of approach with my thumbs stuck in my belt. It is better to start in a softly-softly manner, with confidence and a bit of humour if possible, but never being frightened to ratchet things up if it became necessary.

I left my apartment at about ten o clock that evening with Judith on board. Whilst I had told her to remain in the flat and let me deal with the incident, she insisted on coming. During the journey, I contacted Robert Zolkiewski, who wanted to come with me as well but I needed him back in the control room; I asked him to get my interpreter to the scene urgently. He contacted the local IPTF station commander who also sent two monitors to back me up. I also spoke to Major Chris Powell again, who told me that a whole platoon of soldiers and vehicles were parked up about half a mile away from Kostajnicia and would come as soon as I asked. General Diepenbrugge then came on the radio personally and asked me again if I was sure I didn't want him to intervene. He very kindly agreed to stand aside and give me the first crack at the problem. Knowing that the British army was only half a mile down the road, I felt remarkably reassured.

We drove into the village square close to the bridge over the river Una. I saw the local inhabitants sitting outside in street cafes enjoying the summer evening whilst quaffing local beer and their speciality plum brandy, known as slivovitz (similar to dynamite). Almost simultaneously my interpreter Svetlana arrived and we walked up to the border post where a couple of State Border Service men had been posted. They were both of relatively low rank and unlikely to challenge their orders; no one more senior was present. I noticed that the border post was no more than a portable kiosk with a border crossing sign on a pole in a concrete ten-gallon oil drum. Furthermore, this border crossing had not been operational for years, so the whole thing had no practical point. Svetlana introduced us and I asked the officers why a border post had been established when this crossing was closed. They said they did not know but they were under orders to man it. I then asked why the border post was situated 100m into Croatia; they again replied they did not know but they had orders to stand in this position. I asked who had given the order and they replied, their lieutenant. Realising this matter was being orchestrated by people much higher up the food chain, I informed them that they were on Croatian territory and must pull back one hundred metres. They said they would if they received orders from their officers. I got on to Robert in the control room. I explained the need to get a State Border Service (SBS) senior officer to order these people back. I asked him to get onto our German IPTF monitors who were mainly responsible for building the SBS, as they are world leaders on border policing. As I was speaking, a whole crowd of local villagers swelled out from the square and occupied the narrow strip of land running alongside the castle and up to the bridge over the river Una. A Serbian voice rang out from within their midst in a defiant tone. I turned to Svetlana.

'He says this is their land and they are not moving from it,' she said.

I said, 'Ask him who he is.'

She spoke and a little fat man emerged from the irritable throng and replied (in Serbian) 'I am the mayor and this is our land; we are not moving.'

The hairs pricked up on my head, Bob Gravel was watching me from afar. I had boldly told the military that I could deal with it and it was looking like I was in too deep. To cap it all, David Caudle, a well-nourished German police captain (who I knew well) came on the phone and said, 'There's nothing I can do, Tony; the SBS commanders are not answering their phones!'

It was now clear that this was a plot orchestrated by RS politicians. Try as they might, David Caudle and Robert were unable to raise any senior police officers in the whole of the RS. I phoned Bob Gravel and he was fully aware of the game that was afoot. None of his RS political contacts, to a very senior level were answering their phones.

'Tony, you gotta get those SBS guys to pull back one hundred metres or the Croats are going to send out armed police tomorrow morning to reclaim their territory. You're going to have to fire them if they refuse.'

It was within my power as an IPTF regional commander to recommend to the commissioner that the SBS officers be dismissed from their jobs. By now it was 2am, time had dragged on and none of the villagers seemed to want to return to their beds. I engaged in a long conversation with the SBS officers. I explained the fruitless purpose of a customs and border post on a border that was closed and that they were a part of a scheme which was designed to help the mayor get re-elected by that old game of being brave with other peoples' lives. I also talked about my service in the police and attempted to show that we at least were all policemen and all on the same side. We all have to pay the rent and buy the groceries for our families I stressed. They knew they were pawns in the game and were fully aware that I could recommend their dismissal, which I told them I did not want to do but may have to if they leave me no option. They finally agreed, after a couple of hours of haggling that, if the mayor said it was alright to move the border post back one hundred metres, then they would.

Whilst all these telephone calls and radio messages were being sent and received and during my negotiations with the SBS officers, I had also spent time talking to the fat mayor. He told me that Bill Clinton, the former US President, had made a statement that the borders of all countries ran down the middle of rivers. That is in fact generally true but for some reason of sod's law, in this case the boundary diverted to the southern side of this particular river due to the historic significance of the castle. I entered in long conversations with the mayor who gave me a snapshot of Serbian history and their fight against the Ottoman Empire justifying him in the position he had taken against Croatia. The fact that there was to be a mayoral election in a month's time was not mentioned. I emphasised to him the seriousness of the situation and the need for statesman-like action, I also emphasised that in the end, no matter what it took, this bit of land was going to stay in Croatia. He could generously agree to pull the border back, thus avoiding any loss of face and tell his people that he had done his best but it was up to senior RS politicians to represent the people in this case. The Croats would not reoccupy this small stretch of land until negotiations had concluded, Croat politicians having wisely agreed to keep a low profile for a short while. These factors had the benefit that he could dump this mess into someone else's lap and blame other RS politicians for being soft, whilst he appeared tough. He seemed to be grasping the fact that ultimately this attempt at expanding the border would fail and I was offering a way out whilst preserving his authority. He invited me, Svetlana and Judith to accompany him back to the council chamber at the Town Hall. I then stood on the footplate of my Toyota 4X4 and, balancing precariously, addressed the gathering of villagers with Svetlana's help. I said that the land they were standing on was in dispute with Croatia and their claim was understandable. But I said that this land would still be here in the morning when they woke up and it was a matter for their political leaders to sort out. I also stressed that it was time the two halves of the same village be given a proper crossing so that the families could be reunited.

Judith stayed by my side throughout and was taken on more than one occasion for my interpreter due to her dark complexion and striking good looks. We walked into the council chamber at the town hall where we were met by about twenty or so councillors, most of whom were smoking. The lights were dim and it was like being in a sea fog of cigarette smoke. They seemed a motley bunch; most were wearing suits, they were unshaven and some were wearing sunglasses. By now it was 4am and I felt like I was on a set from *The Godfather*. The mayor addressed his councillors and I was aware of him being questioned closely by some of them; it seemed he was also being backed into a corner by some of these people who were making the bullets for him to fire. However, after some heated exchanges between him and his councillors, he agreed to pull the border post back by a hundred metres and leave it in the hands of senior politicians. We were offered, and drank, several cups of coffee which were most welcome and the meeting ended on very friendly terms. I went back out to the border post and spoke with the SBS officers. They were very relieved that the matter had been resolved and the post was moved back to the official 1995 border. I phoned Bob Gravel, who was delighted about the result and actually even more delighted that I had not, nor was going to, recommend the dismissal of the two SBS men. I saw through a chink in the armour of this highly competent and indeed combative UN professional; he may have been a 'kick ass' North American but he had a huge heart inside his gruff exterior.

Over the next few weeks, the politicians of Croatia, Bosnia and Herzegovina, the UN and others got together; the Foreign Ministers of both countries agreed the precise location of the border which was precisely where it was before the fat mayor was goaded into action by some mischief makers in his own ranks. Just over a month later, I attended the official opening of the border with Dushanka and Fyodor Klimchyk, the UN Russian political advisor who, needless to say, knew everyone who was anyone. We witnessed the first tractor from Croatia trundling over the bridge and passing across the border driven by a fat farmer with his equally fat wife clinging on behind him waving at her relatives on the Bosnian side. I watched the senior politicians in their smart limousines pass through the border in a flourish, including Bob Gravel, as they proceeded to a formal signature signing ceremony with the Croatian Foreign Minister, no doubt followed by a slap up meal. I saw the two SBS officers at their border post who had been there on the night and gave them a wink; they both gave broad grins back. That was a good day in the mission.

Chapter Six
Father Tomislav Matanovic

I tell the next story not because I had a great deal to do with it, but because it needs to be told. Shortly after I arrived in Banja Luka in March 2002, I met Bob Grant who was a former US police officer working as an IPTF monitor on a case involving the murder of a Roman Catholic priest and his family in Prijedor Northern Bosnia in 1995. Bob had been experiencing considerable difficulty in getting the local police in the RS to do anything about it; the fact that the local police had been responsible for the murders may have been a factor.

Bob Grant was an American in his early sixties and had spent all his life in law enforcement. When I met him he was wilting under considerable stress due to the fact that he was having difficulty in persuading the local police to bring charges against the suspects in the case. They were all police personnel, some of whom were still serving and others who were retired. He was convinced that the RS government and senior police officers were protecting the guilty parties. He was dealing with all this on his own and clearly needed backup. This is what he told me.

Fr. Tomislav Matanovic was a Bosnian Croat and Catholic Priest in the region of Prijedor which is situated to the north west of Banja Luka. He was a popular man and when he was ordained in 1989, the congregation included Croatian Catholics, Serbs (mainly Orthodox) and even some Muslim neighbours. He took up his appointment in 1992 and he lived in the Bishop's house in

Banja Luka. For the next three years, he distributed Catholic aid from a variety of donor organisations equally to Catholics, Croats, Serbs and Muslims. He preached remorselessly against the large scale eviction and displacement of the Muslims which became known as ethnic cleansing. The stand he took against these actions drew him powerful enemies. Bosnian Serb politicians, using their leverage over the local police, decided to act. In Bosnia at that time and in many other countries, politicians exerted considerable influence and control over the police which resulted in the political enemies of the ruling party being singled out, harassed, imprisoned and murdered. It is fundamental in a free society that the police retain operational control without political interference and the public must always remain vigilant to protect this principal.

On 24 August 1995, four months before the end of the war at the Dayton peace accords signed 14 December 1995, Fr Matanovic and his father, Josip, were arrested by the RS Prijedor police at his parsonage near the church and taken to Urije police station within the Prijedor region. At the police station, they were interrogated by members of the crime police. The parsonage was systematically searched and looted. All valuable material including cash raised for Caritas, the Roman Catholic aid and development agency, was stolen and the parish hall was demolished with heavy machinery.

At 12.30am the following day, Fr. Matanovic and his father were taken to the Matanovic family home where they were detained between 25 August to 19 September. They were guarded by the police and no one had access to them. During this period of detention, Fr. Matanovic was repeatedly questioned by the Prijedor crime police and his family home was looted. On the 19 September, at around 2.00am Fr. Matanovic, his father and his mother, Bozena, who were both in their seventies, disappeared from the family home and none of them were ever seen alive again. They had been under the close confinement of the Prijedor police throughout and it is suspected they were all murdered within hours of their removal from their house.

On 21 December and again on 23 March 1996, the authorities

of the Republika Srbska offered to exchange Fr. Tomislav Matanovic and his parents for prisoners of war held by the Federation of Bosnia and Herzegovina. This was a cynical and callous act because all three had probably been murdered the previous September. In 1996, the UN Human Rights Chamber rendered a decision on the merits of the case and found the government of the RS responsible for the disappearance of the Matanovic family.[3] An RS police investigation began in 1996, but the RS government were allegedly complicit in obstructing this investigation, which ended in failure. During the civil war, almost four thousand Bosniaks and Croats disappeared from the Prijedor area, either evicted from their homes or murdered; the police were said to be deeply involved in the ethnic cleansing.

With the establishment of the UN IPTF in 2001, a second Ministry of Interior investigation team was formed. This team quickly found Fr. Matanovic's motor car at the traffic police station in Prijedor and documentation was seized which showed that the car had been illegally confiscated. Senior RS police officers were found to have been involved in the seizure of this vehicle, including the special advisor to Simo Drljaca, the public security centre (police station) commander for Prijedor. He had been subject to an arrest warrant issued in 1997 by the ICTY, in that, as a member of the Crisis Committee for Prijedor he was complicit in the ethnic cleansing of Muslims and ethnic Croats plus the torture of detainees at the Prijedor public security centre. He was further alleged to be involved in the administration of the Omarska prison camp and other facilities nearby. Four police officers were identified as being involved in the illegal detention of the Matanovic family and were dismissed from their posts by the IPTF commissioner. This second RS police investigation team found it difficult to accept that the Matanovic family had been held illegally, preferring to use the term 'secured'.

On 19 July 1997, Simo Drljaca was spotted near the Gradine lake near Omarska. This was near the site of the notorious internment camp where half-starved prisoners were photographed during the civil war and which appeared in newspapers around the world showing pictures of emaciated men and boys. He was alleged by ICTY to have helped in the establishment and running of this detention facility. He was challenged as he walked near the lake by British SAS special forces soldiers who had been lying in wait for him. Drljaca ran away from them fearing he would be arrested and sent to The Hague; he turned and discharged his hand gun at them as he ran. The soldiers returned fire and he was killed instantly, the autopsy on his body revealing that three of the soldiers' bullets had each tracked through his heart from separate directions. Authorities in the RS claimed that he was murdered. With the man who almost certainly approved and orchestrated the abduction of Fr. Tomislav and his family now dead, it remained to find their killers and abductors.

In September 2001, the bodies of Fr. Tomislav, his father and mother were all found decomposed at the bottom of a well near the village of Bišćani, outside Prijedor, by Bosnian Muslim refugees who were returning home. Forensic tests identified the bodies as Father Matanovic and his parents. Fr. Tomislav and Josip were handcuffed with RS police issue handcuffs.[4] All had been shot in the head; Josip and Bozena from behind, but Fr. Tomislav had been shot between the eyes from the front. The last thing he probably saw was both his parents being shot and then the executioner placing the gun against his forehead. Forensic evidence was said to show that all three had been killed by handguns, a bullet with a calibre of 7.65 mm as used by the RS police being found in the skull of Fr. Tomislav.

Bob Grant continued to work almost singlehandedly and monitored the local police investigation. He helped arrange ballistics tests on all police handguns found at Prijedor police station. He also, and with considerable effort, arranged for all policemen who worked at that station during 1995 to submit to polygraph tests. These are in effect lie detector tests based on blood pressure, pulse, respiration and skin perspiration carried out by trained operators. As a result of Bob's efforts, together with further assistance given by additional UN staff, a number of serving and former RS policemen were identified as being involved in the illegal detention of the Matanovic family. My only claim to have helped in this matter was to give Bob extra staff which I did; this had the effect of easing his burden and sharing the responsibility.

In January 2003, eleven former policemen were charged with crimes in connection with this illegal detention. The responsibility for prosecuting the men lay with the judicial authorities in the RS; it was not a matter for the International Criminal Court. The proceedings commenced in May 2004 and on 11 February 2005 all suspects stood trial for the illegal detention of Fr. Tomislav and his family. The court in Prijedor acquitted all eleven defendants, citing lack of evidence as the reason. None of the former police officers have ever been charged with the murders. I was the regional commander in Banja Luka during the closing stages of the investigation into these murders. There was little or no pressure applied by RS politicians or the local press on their police to carry out a thorough investigation. In fact, from the perspective of many internationals working in the region, it was almost certain that ways would be found to acquit the accused. Having worked on investigations for over thirty years, I found it hard to stomach that the local police with eleven suspects could possibly fail to bring the offenders to court with the necessary evidence. People talk and accused persons will squeal to try to reduce the sentences against them; that is, of course, unless they are being protected by persons in high places. In February 2016, Bosnia and Herzegovina applied to join the European Union; they will need to support their application by demonstrating that they can and are dealing with the sins of the past committed by their own people against their own people. Another investigation by the Ministry of Interior of the Republika Srbska in co-operation with the chief prosecutor commenced in October 2011.

Fr. Matanovic was a true Christian martyr who died for his faith in the service of his fellow man, whatever their religion or ethnicity. He and his family are just three out of a total of 40,000 people who went missing as a consequence of armed conflict in the former Yugoslavia of which 30,000 were from Bosnia. 14,000 remain unaccounted for and the International Committee of the

Red Cross (ICRC) estimates that this affects the lives of 200,000 people. These families have also been denied justice.[5]

I last saw Bob Grant several years later at Camp Victory in Baghdad, a vast US fortification around the airbase. He was working on a programme to train the Iraqi police. I saw an axe handle sticking out of his rucksack. 'What's that, Bob?' I asked.

'A fighting axe,' he replied. 'If I run out of ammo, I've got that.' In his mid-sixties, he was still a formidable and all-American boy.

Chapter Seven
Human Trafficking

When I first arrived in Bosnia, the UN were pursuing a vigorous programme to combat the trafficking of human beings, who in this case were almost all exclusively women from Eastern Europe going to, or being taken to Bosnia, to work in the sex trade. The four years of civil war had left the country struggling with shattered and dysfunctional institutions, lack of commerce, high unemployment, poverty, homelessness on a vast scale, corruption and rampant crime. Add to this thousands of international soldiers, mainly young men full of testosterone, military contractors and international humanitarian organisations comprising many men away from home with pockets stuffed full of dollars and it is not surprising that poor women and opportunistic men will move into this explosive and exploitative mix. The vast bulk of the internationals wanted to help a poor, abused and war-weary people, but there will always be those few who succumb to a baser instinct and try to internally justify it.

On 25 July 2001, the United Nations Mission in Bosnia and Herzegovina (UNMIBH) established a programme called the Special Trafficking Operations Programme, hereafter called STOP, to combat human trafficking. When I arrived in the mission in October of that year, this fight against human trafficking was well under way. The IPTF provided 53 international police officers to this project who in turn monitored the work of 150 Bosnian police men and women stationed in different parts of the country. I was surprised to learn that this programme did not come under the management or control of the IPTF Commissioner Brigadier-General Coeurderoy, but was run by a UN French civilian, Celhia de Laverne. I understood that she was a trained journalist and was considered an expert in human trafficking. Before I had been deployed to the mission, there had been several scandals involving IPTF policemen visiting brothels, locally called 'night clubs', which had caused considerable embarrassment to the UNMIBH and had been highlighted in the international press. There were also serious allegations that members of the UN, including IPTF monitors, were more than just customers in these brothels but also involved in organising and facilitating the trade. I took a very strong stance on this issue from the start and briefed all my officers plus new arrivals over the next twelve months that if they were caught in a brothel, then there was only one decision for them to make; do they want an aisle seat or a window seat for the trip home? Fortunately, this was never a decision that had to be made by a British officer during my time in Bosnia.

I had little to do with this aspect of the mission's work until I took up my post as regional commander at Banja Luka. I had seven IPTF stations under my command, all of which were commanded by international police officers generally of major (or chief inspector) rank. These IPTF stations monitored the work of the local police in the districts in which they were situated. My station commanders were from Pakistan, Waseem, a born optimist; Spain, Carlos Castro, another outstanding policeman; and five others, including an excellent Argentinian who I had selected on an interview over an English candidate. As I settled in at Banja Luka, my deputy, Robert Zolkiewski, told me that the main problem affecting the running of the region was the activity of the STOP teams, who he described as like a private army answering to no one other than Ms de Laverne and conducting themselves like prima donnas. Over the next couple of months, I received complaints about three separate incidents which included a British constable STOP team member ordering my Spanish major to provide vehicles and then to transport some women found in a brothel to Sarajevo. Major Castro said he would try his best as he didn't have enough vehicles but the British constable shouted down the phone that he wouldn't try, he would do it! Major Castro was taken back by this dictatorial and disrespectful treatment and complained to me about it. A similar complaint was made by another of my officers who complained that another British constable STOP team member had shouted at him during a night club raid, that he should not be present on the raid and emphasised what he was saying by pointing his finger at him, 'treating me like a delinquent,' the aggrieved officer said. This outburst occurred in the presence of subordinates, which had the effect of totally humiliating him and undermining his authority. I received further complaints about the activity of this group who seemed to be acting like tin gods, commanding officers of senior rank to them, with none of the skills of command, acting without discipline and outside the chain of command.

I was determined to restore order and try and get back some professionalism into the running of this region. I started by calling together all of the officers who were making complaints and interviewing them to satisfy myself of the accuracy of their accounts. I also sought to obtain witnesses who could corroborate their stories, if true, which I did. This kind of arrogant dictatorial behaviour was happening not only in Banja Luka but all over the mission area, according to what other fellow regional commanders were telling me.

I then managed to get hold of internal UN reports which outlined the achievements of the STOP team in Banja Luka between April 2001 and April 2002. I discovered that they had raided 24 night clubs, checked over a 110 females and deported (in the words of the BiH Department of Foreigners) 79 women. The UN STOP team in their press briefings used the words 'rescued' rather than deported. All those deported were using false or forged passports and came principally from Moldova, the poorest country in Europe, and Romania. Of the women 'rescued' or 'deported' there were a greater number who had told police officers when their clubs were raided that they were content in their employment and wished to stay in Bosnia. This push by the international community against trafficking in human beings appeared to me to be some kind of crusade and backed up with statistics which were quite astronomical; for example, the Centre for Research of Democracy reported that there were 1000 brothels in Bosnia with over 15,000 women working in them. However, for the same time period, the RS Ministry of Interior reported that in the RS (making up roughly one-fifth the size of the whole country) the numbers of brothels stood at eight with twenty-three women working in them.

Next one has to ask the question 'what is trafficking?' Well, it is defined by the United Nations Office on Drugs and Crime (UNODC) as the recruitment, transportation, transfer, harbouring or receipt of persons, by means of the threat or use of force or other forms of coercion. This includes abduction, or by deception, (for example the promise of well-paid bar work without reference to prostitution) for the purpose of exploitation. Exploitation shall include, at a minimum, the exploitation of the prostitution of others or other forms of sexual exploitation, forced labour or services, slavery or practices similar to slavery, servitude or the removal of organs.[6]

I was certainly aware of cases where this was true and on one occasion in my region two women escaped from a brothel, one of whom had cut her wrists and was taken to hospital. Fortunately, the medical staff telephoned the local police who in turn told their IPTF interlocutors. One of the women told the officers who were called that she had been kept as a prisoner in the night club or brothel by being locked in a bedroom and had been forced to engage in sexual intercourse with up to fifteen men a night. Some of the women found in the STOP team raids were truly rescued in these operations and this example is not unique. The problem is that life is not black and white and there were significant numbers of women who came from desperately poor families in Eastern Europe, who were prepared to engage in prostitution and make as much money as they could. The skill is in finding out which ones are the real trafficking victims and focussing police resources not only on rescuing those women but taking the perpetrators out of the game through prosecution and imprisonment, thus stopping them from causing further misery. I was not convinced that sufficient investigative work was being conducted to achieve these ends by the blunt tactics used by the STOP teams. To illustrate this point, I established that between April 2001 and April 2002 none of the bar owners of the brothels raided in the RS had received a sentence of imprisonment.

Whilst digging into all this chaos, I was approached by a British female officer working on a STOP team who told me that she was going to be taking part in a raid on a club where the bar owner was suspected of being in possession of illegal firearms. She had made representations within her unit that the operation would be too dangerous to carry out by unarmed officers, but no heed was taken of her concerns. I agreed with her that, as the information about the bar owner appeared to have some substance, an armed operation should be carried out first and the premises made safe, after which the STOP team would enter with the local police and do their work. I told her to advise her management that I did not approve of the raid without neutralising the risk posed by a bar owner with an AK47 first. She attempted to cancel the raid but was told that the operation had to proceed because the press were going to be present that night. She told me that within the unit there was a lot of playing to the (press) gallery. In view of what she told me, I overrode the STOP team management and withdrew her from the raid. This had the effect of maintaining my low popularity ratings with some members of the STOP teams.

With all this in mind, I wrote to Brigadier-General Coeurderoy to complain about the manner in which station commanders in my region were being treated by members of the STOP teams and of other procedural irregularities including the appointment of translators – a well-paid job for Bosnians – by ignoring the proper fair selection procedures and trying to appoint their local 'friends' to positions in their units. My High Command sent me back a reply saying that it was politically dangerous for me to criticise the STOP teams, they were outside the IPTF chain of command and I was to 'be careful'. I also heard on the grapevine from my trusty Polish Major Robert, that one of the STOP team members was putting it about that Celhia and the Special Representative of the Secretary General Jacques Paul Kline were organising an enquiry to have me repatriated to the UK because of my interfering. Needless to say, I doubt that such senior people in the mission were aware that I existed at all. This manufacturing of malicious rumours was typical of some members of that unit who were consumed by their own magnificence.

Fortunately, not long after this episode, the STOP team at Banja Luka got a new team leader in the form of Sergeant Padraig de Burca from the Guarda Sochna in the Republic of Ireland. Padraig was an accomplished sergeant of the type with which I am familiar. He kept me updated on issues regarding the activities of the team, even inviting me along on a raid or two. I distinctly remember one of the night clubs we raided in Banja Luka. It was a seedy place, where, when you put the lights on, all the decaying decor and indeed decaying people could be clearly seen. The bar owner was a large, fat, unwashed man with bad teeth. Behind the bar, one of the STOP team had found a rubber hose pipe, about one foot in length, loaded with ball bearings and sealed at both ends, about which he was being questioned. Two young women with somewhat pimply complexions were standing in the centre of the small main room which measured about twenty feet by twenty feet. They were being spoken to by local police and STOP team members. They both came from Moldova and appeared embarrassed; they seemed to have that look on their faces which said, 'Don't tell my mother'. There were only a few middle aged men in the night club and again, they also had that look of embarrassment. One of them had a lot more reason than the others to be embarrassed, because he was a locally employed driver for the UNMIBH and had parked his marked UN vehicle smack outside the club. I took it upon myself to deal with this internal disciplinary matter as the STOP team and local police were there to deal with crimes involving trafficking. The UN driver quickly came forward after I had asked our interpreter to tell him to make himself known. The next day, I discreetly told his head of department and he was quietly fired. Had all STOP team members been of the quality of Padraig, then not only would there have been far fewer problems, but more bad men may have been put out of circulation. The young women in this raid both said that they were working freely for the bar owner and did not request assistance from the UN. The Department for Foreigners found all their documents to be in order.

2002 was the final year of UNMIBH. From the beginning of January 2003, a new organisation took over from the UN in the form of the European Union Police Mission (EUPM) which was headed by Sven Fredericksen, a giant Dane both in stature and personality. I applied for a job with the EUPM as I had been due to retire from the Dorset Police at the end of that year. Fortunately, I had a lot of institutional knowledge having been there a year, I got the plum job of 'Senior Advisor on Major and Organised Crime' plus I had a staff of senior European detectives to help me. One of my briefs was to organise an anti-human-trafficking department. The UN had 1,795 police personnel and an executive mandate, whilst the EUPM were going to have 500 police officers in total. We would not have the luxury of having fifty-three European police officers to deploy against human traffickers, but I did have two Dutch police officers in the form of Maria Donk and Zoltan Pap joining the European mission and what we lacked in numbers we made up for in quality. Maria and Zoltan were highly experienced; Maria worked at Schiphol Airport, with previous service on the vice squad and Zoltan headed the anti-trafficking department in Amsterdam. They both came out to Bosnia as the UN mission was winding down to set up the Human Trafficking Department with me for the EUPM. I wanted our effort with the local police in this field to be an 'intelligence-led' approach and I needed several things. One of these was a better grip for the new mission on criminal intelligence held by the local police throughout the country. I was luckily in a position to be able to convince Commissioner Fredericksen and his new deputy Philippe Miailhes of the French gendarmerie, both very practical coppers, that we needed to have a European middle-ranking officer in each of the ten canton intelligence offices, one or two in the RS, a similar number in the federal Ministry of Interior and one or two in the State Border Service and Brcko. And so it was that the infrastructure to develop the model of intelligence-led policing with the local police was laid in place. We had in effect stitched it all together and could see the whole picture of criminal intelligence across the country from a high vantage point.

The next thing we needed in order to continue the fight against human trafficking was to acquire the wealth of intelligence information the UN STOP teams had accumulated since their inception in June 2001. With this, we could start to carry out detailed analysis of criminals, their associates, vehicles, registration numbers, phone numbers, addresses, prostitutes, deported females and genuine rescued trafficking victims. All this data is the bread and butter of any criminal intelligence data base. Each small piece, sometimes innocuous, builds up to complete a picture giving the overall view of a criminal network. Now I thought, in my naivety, that with all the work and publicity given to this type of crime by the UN, that to be handed all this data for the purpose of continuing the fight against this insidious crime would be a formality. It was anything but and the obstruction I got was breath-taking in its arrogance.

In mid-December 2002, which was the last month of the UN mission before the EUPM took over the following January, a letter was received from the UN which stated that certain files would be made available to the new mission. These included the investigations into the Travnik murders I had earlier been involved in overseeing, plus a number of other high profile and ongoing investigations, which included open and closed STOP team files. It took the UN until April 2003 to copy some of these files and make them available to the EUPM, but no STOP team files were included in this tranche of material. The UN would not release the files to the new mission but made them available for inspection; this was far from ideal. We waited and waited and it was not until May 2003, after repeated requests from myself and Zoltan, that the STOP team files arrived and when they did certain key cases were excluded, including ones from Prijedor which involved IPTF police monitors being found in brothels. We needed the files for several months in our possession so that we could extract all the intelligence. I personally knew the head of the ICTY investigation team in Sarajevo, Jan Van Hecke and he told me he would be willing to hold these files for us and was very sympathetic to our need for this intelligence material. On 13 May 2003, he wrote to the UN with this offer to store the files in Sarajevo. I wrote to the UN the same month to ask for files in relation to a major criminal who I was particularly interested in as I wanted an operation mounted on him. He was Milorad Milakovic, who I understood operated a 'night club' in Prijedor. I did not receive a reply and when the files arrived I had Zoltan and Maria search them, but there was nothing to be found on Milakovic whatsoever. As ICTY had not received a reply either I was getting concerned, because I wanted to build our data base as quickly as possible. Accordingly, therefore, I sent Zoltan and Maria to the room in the UN building in Sarajevo where these files were stored to extract as much information as they could. They devised a form to focus their search on phone numbers, associates, vehicles and so on.

Between May to mid-June Zoltan and Maria obtained over 200 pro forma sheets on offenders, suspects, associates, prostitutes and victims. The key to the room was held by a local UN employee who was surly and frequently kept Zoltan and Maria waiting for long periods before she would give them the key to the room. I went to see her personally about the obstruction she was giving with the intention of smoothing things over. I asked her if she knew where the files concerning the Milakovic family were being kept. She told me that we could not have access to them, we had 'no right' she retorted; she told me that she had worked with the STOP teams and 'was I surprised the files were missing?' It was slowly beginning to dawn on me that it seemed some people in the UN didn't want the EUPM to succeed in the fight against trafficking. In early June, I went on holiday leaving Maria and Zoltan to plough through the files. On the 22 June 2003 I returned from leave, to be told by a distraught Maria that the UN had destroyed all the human trafficking material. The person responsible for keeping the files was a Mr. Setian, a UN administrator, who told her that the material had been destroyed. He added that the EUPM had had six months to look at them. This was of course completely untrue and he must have known that, as they had only been made available in May and we had been given access for less than six weeks. I went personally to see Mr Setian and asked him if the STOP team files were there.

When I asked, he replied 'No, they've all been destroyed.'

I said, 'Why?'

He replied, 'That's not for you to bloody ask!' The man was bubbling with rage as I entered his office and was very aggressive. I told him that ICTY were willing to hold the files for the EUPM and he replied that he was unaware of that and because he had not had a reply from New York he had destroyed them. Needless to say, I was devastated at this loss of intelligence material. To make matters worse, he seemed to have a triumphal attitude about denying to another international organisation material that would have been used to fight human trafficking.

All the material destroyed included vital information in English; much of which had been translated from the local language. Also included in the files were photographs of some of the main players. It would have cost countless thousands of pounds to pay for the translations alone, not to mention the policing skills needed to acquire the material in the first place. Our fight against human trafficking and organised crime suffered a serious setback and it took us much longer to build up this quality and quantity of information than should have been necessary. We were never offered electronic copies of this material, much of which was stored on UN computers; this again would have helped enormously.

The UN in the early days of UNPROFOR,[7] SFOR and then the UNMIBH did outstanding work in the cause of peace for which many peace keepers of all nationalities both military and civilian gave their lives. UNMIBH was an unqualified success which rebuilt fractured institutions, particularly the criminal justice sector. Industry and commerce bring employment and wealth to many people, but before a state can prosper it needs to provide security through the rule of law, only then can true reconstruction begin; and the UN delivered. So why after all the publicity and high profile activities of the STOP team were these files destroyed? Why were they not handed direct to the EUPM? Why were they not handed into the care of ICTY? Could Mr Setian, a mid- ranking UN administrator, have had the authority to destroy this criminal intelligence information without reference to someone more senior? Was it gross incompetence by an organisation whose administrative procedures were second to none, or was it something else? Did someone want the EUPM to fail in the fight against human trafficking? Were egos and careers more important than working in partnership with other organisations to combat this evil? Whatever the answer may be, it is clear to me that the destruction of this intelligence material was more than just a misunderstanding.

Chapter Eight

Milorad Milakovic
'They sell footballs don't they?'

The first time that I had become aware of the name Milorad Milakovic was not long after I had taken up my post as regional commander in Banja Luka in February 2002. Robert Zolkiewski, my deputy, took me on a drive around the region and we went to the IPTF Station in Prijedor to meet Waseem, the IPTF station commander. During the journey, Robert pointed out to me a hotel which resembled a castle with crenulated battlements atop a cement stucco wall. It all looked pretty tacky but was well fortified with high walls and tall iron gates. Robert told me that it was owned by Milorad Milakovic, who he described to me as mafia. It was rumoured that he had a couple of tigers penned up in a cage in a quadrangle within the building. He said Milakovic was involved in a lot of prostitution in the area and that there had been a big scandal a couple of years ago, approximately the summer of 2000, when about six IPTF monitors had either been caught there or found in other brothels in the area. They had apparently been repatriated back to their countries of origin. There had been talk of an American IPTF monitor or Department of Defence (DOD) contractor 'buying' a woman from one of these brothels and keeping her in his flat. He apparently later said that he wanted to 'save her' from a life of prostitution. It seemed more like he wanted to save her for himself. All this to me at the time was rumour and speculation, I had seen nothing official about all this, but it put some 'meat on the bones' concerning the message I got from the commissioner to 'be careful.' For the rest of that year, I kept myself aware of any reports concerning this individual, but as trafficking in human beings was the domain of the STOP teams I instigated no action. When I learned that the EUPM would be taking over in January 2003, he came into my thinking as potentially a good target for the local police to develop, so I kept him simmering on my mental cooker.

In 2003, an article appeared in the *National Geographic* magazine which was written by a very brave journalist Andrew Cockburn.[8] He described how he had travelled alone to the Sherwood Hotel one grey spring morning, where he had met Milorad Milakovic who he described as a burly 54-year-old. Milakovic told the reporter that prostitution should be legalised, because the selling of people was wrong and the women were all someone's child. This was a very caring approach from a man who was earlier attributed with making statements to a human rights activist such as, 'Is it a crime to sell women? They sell footballers don't they?' He threatened to kill this activist but took a softer tone with Mr Cockburn. There were several burly men about the place and Cockburn noticed a trio of what he described as 'Serbian tigers' prowling in a compound.

The EUPM was under considerable pressure to demonstrate publicly that the fight against human trafficking would continue with vigour as had been displayed by the UN. This pressure in turn was transferred onto my shoulders with the requirement to produce some high profile operation to keep the press happy. This was not at all my style, but I produced one large scale operation to be conducted by the local police, with their prosecutors, accompanied by EUPM monitors on known brothels. The raids were duly conducted in mid-January 2003, with the result that my senior management were kept happy, as were the press. But I was not at all happy. It involved too many EUPM monitors, too many local police and too few prosecutions; and none for anything which could be considered 'organised crime'.[9] I wrote a report to Commissioner Sven Fredericksen, in which I stressed that we must stick to an 'intelligence-led policing approach', using a surgeon's knife to the infection rather than a blunt hammer to everything. The approach would be one of 'partnership', which was a buzz word of the times, but it works. The prevention and detection of crime is not solely a police responsibility and in the international arena even less so. This was going to take the full commitment of the local police, commitment from politicians of BiH and the co-operation of myriad international organisations, each with their own expertise and capability.

I worked hard with Maria and Zoltan to speak to the polyglot of organisations working in Bosnia who contributed any input in the field of the trafficking of human beings. What I found out was that there was a lot of expertise out there. We met with the International Organisation for Migration (IOM), who ran an anti-human trafficking programme funded by the US government. They were willing to help in providing secure refuges for trafficking victims and these centres would be available all times of the night and day so that the EUPM could take victims there after a successful operation. IOM were running and managing safe houses all over Bosnia and they would even take self-confessed prostitutes if there was the slightest possibility they could be persuaded out of the life they had got themselves into. We also met an English lawyer, Madeline Rees, who worked for the United Nations High Commission for Human Rights as the gender expert and Head of Office in Bosnia and Herzegovina. She would also prove to be an invaluable find for me as she would in due course obtain a place of refuge for trafficking victims in an enlightened European country but not the country of origin of the victim; known as 'third country repatriation'. We also met with the Organisation for Co-operation and Security in Europe (OSCE) who again were enthusiastic and helpful. The most important group of people were the Bosnians themselves. The state prosecutor, my (now) old friend Marinko Durcevic, gave his full commitment. He knew the law better than anyone and suggested that the political leadership pass a law giving a temporary permit of leave to remain in BiH for women who would give evidence in court. This was achieved with full commitment from the BiH Council of Ministers. The local police, seeing the involvement of the state prosecutor, were cognisant of his leadership and gave their full enthusiastic co-operation; it looked like the only way was up.

One key man I also met in my bid to join up all the resources into one synchronised machine was Lt Colonel Kern Malin. He was a very ballsy, 'hands on' British army colonel in charge of the Royal Military Police (RMP). I had met him on one of my visits to the Metal Factory in Banja Luka in mid-January of 2003. I discussed my organised crime strategy with him as I wanted his input and he offered British army assistance in training the local police in certain surveillance tactics. At the same time, we talked about local crime in the region, including Mr Milakovic, over a plate of fish and chips in the mess, a speciality of the British army on campaign.

Due entirely to his efforts and drive, at 0500 on Wednesday morning the 26 February 2003, he led his troops on a number of raids of four premises in the RS. He used the army's authority under 'Operation Harvest' to seize and recover illegally held weapons. You would be forgiven for thinking that he may have had other things in mind. One of the places raided was the Sherwood Hotel; the other three premises raided were brothels belonging to Milorad Milakovic. The RMP found, within the Sherwood Hotel Milka Milakovic, the middle aged wife of Milorad, and her bodyguard Stoyac. More importantly, they recovered a goldmine of material which comprised twenty-five sacks of documents containing over thirty photocopies of passports of foreign women, documents and copies of medical examinations of over 200 women, one nine mm pistol registered to Milka and one CZ Glock 9 mm pistol which was unregistered, plus ammunition for other hand guns. There were also photographs of local RS police men who were *not* corrupt, so that bouncers and other Milakovic 'employees' would know who to watch out for. A Banja Luka Municipality official rubber stamp was also found by the RMP, which we later discovered had been used to forge official papers. Accounting documents pertaining to nine brothels were also recovered which included a charging rate of 50 KM for sex. The 'Convertible Mark' was the currency in BiH at the time and pegged to the German mark. Fifty KM was about 25 Euros; or 35 US dollars or £21.00.

Of the photographs found, one showed Stoyac posing with one of the seized hand guns, a nice piece of evidence. Another photograph recovered from the Sherwood Hotel showed a drunk and insensible man in the uniform of a UN IPTF monitor from an African country. The background of the photograph showed it to have been taken in one of the Milakovic family's brothels. In addition to this excellent work, the RMP had recorded and labelled every document, photograph, firearms and ammunition in accordance with the rules of evidence to the standard of a British court. No smart lawyer would be able to get their client off the hook on a technicality, like a failure in the continuity of the exhibit or chain of custody. Once all the recovered property and documents had been itemised, Lt Col Malin contacted me and handed over the lot. He was fully aware that it was the responsibility of the local police and prosecutor to investigate and that we in the EUPM would do our best to make sure that dark forces would be prevented from scuppering the investigation. I was deeply indebted to him and his soldiers. Milka and Stoyac were not arrested by the military and Milorad was nowhere to be found.

My next task was to find some EUPM monitors up to the task of working with the local police on the investigation of this organised crime family. It was again my good fortune that amongst my team was Jean Philippe Plassard, a French captain of gendarmes, with whom I worked well. I discussed the case with him and he found a French detective from Marseilles for me, Jean Pierre, an expert investigator in the field of organised crime. We set up a separate office for Jean Pierre and I found another French EUPM policeman to work with him and importantly, I managed to obtain two interpreters to start reducing all these papers into English so we could see exactly what we had.

The next stop with my French investigators was the office of Mr. Jetimovac, Banja Luka PSC Chief and Milorad Jelisavac, Chief of CID. I knew Mr Jelisavac well as I had taken him and other

Bosnian Police officers, including my old friend Anto Simic, on a visit to Scotland Yard and my county police force in Dorset the previous year. I outlined the case and the action taken by the RMP and details of the material they had recovered. I requested that the RS police set up an investigation team to catalogue and make enquiries regarding the wealth of evidence recovered. They both agreed and were concerned about the need for secrecy and, above all, officers who could be trusted. They well knew that the Milakovic organised crime family had tentacles everywhere. For the next three months, five experienced RS officers and the French detectives worked hard following up the leads found in the documents which had been seized.

Chapter Nine
The Milakovic Mafia

During the three months following the search by the RMP and subsequent action which occurred in May 2003, a picture of this crime family was constructed. In 1996, just after the end of the civil war in the former Yugoslavia, the authorities in the RS noticed a build-up of foreign women working in the region. In October 1997, a Ukrainian woman escaped from the Maskarada (Masquerade) night club run by Sasa Milakovic, the son of Milorad and Milka, and she made a statement to the police describing how she had been held in slavery and forced to perform sexual acts with paying customers at the club. She was found by the local health authority to be HIV positive and was repatriated to the Ukraine, with an additional order that she was not to return to Bosnia for three years. As a result of her deportation she could not attend court and give evidence and as a consequence further action was not taken against Sasa following her allegations.

This pattern was repeated over the next few years, with foreign women escaping from brothels in the region and making allegations against the Milakovic family. In 1998, seven foreign females were repatriated from the family's brothels and in 1999, Milka was charged with intimidating foreign women at the Crazy Horse and Paradiso clubs, but the case collapsed. In 1999, the UN IPTF raided the Maskarada night club and interviewed twelve women who were all repatriated; once again, the prime witnesses were not in Bosnia long enough to testify in court. In early 2000, three women were caught illegally exiting the country at a border post in Beilina. They explained that they were escaping from forced prostitution at the Maskarada night club. No statement was taken from them; instead they were redirected to a more lax border crossing. Later the same year, five foreign women made statements alleging rape and forced prostitution against members of the Milakovic family and their gang but no prosecutions resulted. Interestingly, the women quoted the price for full sex at 50 KM, as shown on documents seized from the Sherwood Hotel by the RMP. Again, in June 2001, a woman came forward to the local police in the RS to make an allegation of rape and human trafficking against Sasa but no action was taken.

Why were all these different women from different night clubs making the same sort of allegations to different law enforcement officials, in different parts of the RS at different times but not ending in successful prosecutions against this family? The answer of course is a mixture of corruption, threats and use of extreme violence. In 2003, the new RS police investigation team uncovered witnesses who saw Milka taking drinks and gifts to the RS Department for Foreigners, who were responsible for regulating these foreign women. Certain public officials were visitors to the family's night clubs where they enjoyed free sex with the women. Several people came forward and made statements describing how they were threatened with execution by Sasa, who was in possession of a hand gun. Some of these people were terrified of Sasa, who they said was a psychopath and had been a paramilitary during the civil war. He was also implicated by other witnesses in the extortion of money from local people. The family ruled by a combination of bribery, threats and sexual favours. However, as the criminal organisation grew in its audacity, so it attracted equal animosity in the opposite direction from the local people it was intimidating. This collision course resulted in local people coming forward and making demands on the local authorities to take action. A petition was handed in to the mayor's office signed by prominent citizens of Prijedor, begging that action be taken against this crime family for their open criminality and threats. Some of these citizens worked at the local health centre in Prijedor and were subject to threats and intimidation from Slavisa Milakovic, another son, who paid them a visit after he had found out about the petition

Things then took an even more insidious turn. In April 2003, as a part of the ongoing investigation, the RS police checked a Volkswagen Golf motor car registered to Niko Arsenic, a laboratory assistant in the blood transfusion department at the health centre in Doboj, a town in northern Bosnia about 100 miles to the east of Prijedor. In the vehicle were found blank and completed medical examination records in relation to foreign women employed in the Milakovic family brothels. These medical records were signed by Drs Biljana and Torbica Djurkocic, who both worked at the Doboj Health Centre. When the medical records were shown to Dr Biljana, she stated adamantly that the signatures were not hers; they were, in fact, forgeries. The doctors did not recognise the names of the females on the medical forms and some of the medical certificates bore the name of a doctor who didn't work in the Doboj health centre at all. Niko Arsenic soon discovered that the police had visited Dr Biljana Djurkocic and learned what she had told the police; he confronted her about this and she told him that she had made a statement about the forged documents. He was furious and assaulted her there and then in the Health Centre. She ran to her manager and complained to him about the assault by Niko, plus his unauthorised possession of documents and hospital stamps. She was rewarded for her troubles by her contract not being extended and no disciplinary action being taken against Niko Arsenic by the Health Centre management.

Now, why are all these medical records, blank medical records and so on important? The answer is, because they gave a clean bill of health to the women working in the Milakovic brothels. When the women's medical conditions were re-examined, without Arsenic falsifying records, some of the women were found to be suffering from HIV/AIDs and syphilis. The fact of the matter was that luring these women to Bosnia from neighbouring countries and accompanying them for the whole journey, plus smuggling them through borders, bribing officials and conditioning them to work in sexual slavery had cost the family time and money; they just wanted to keep their overheads down! It was just business to them. The tentacles of the Milakovic family reached everywhere and their complete disregard for everybody in the area was of enormous destructive effect.

As time drew on after the raids by the RMP, my French colleagues and I kept a close watch on the enquiry. I was sure that Mr Jetimovac was an uncorrupted and very professional police officer who would have only deployed to this investigation police officers who could be trusted. However, I was worried that with the corroding reach of this family their tentacles may in some way penetrate this enquiry and derail it. After all, despite the number of allegations made by women who escaped from the family's brothels and several raids on their 'night clubs' in years gone by, they had always evaded prosecution and I believe they thought this time would be no different. Fortunately, I worked closely with George Mills, a member of the British 'Serious Fraud Office' who, as the name implies, dealt with national level major fraud cases in the UK. George was on secondment to the Office of the High Representative (OHR) who between 2004 and 2008 was Lord 'Paddy' Ashdown, former leader of the Liberal Democrat Party and a former Royal Marine. George had a close working relationship with the prosecutors in BiH and in particular with Mr Durcevic the state prosecutor. I think we were all gravely concerned that if this investigation stayed in Banja Luka or Prijedor there would be a serious or even successful attempt to sink the prosecution case because of this family's pervasive reach.

Our suspicions did not have long to ferment because on 8 May 2003, Milorad Milakovic answered a request from the police to attend Banja Luka PSC to clear up a few points. To his utter surprise, he was arrested and detained and the local police set out to search his home, the Sherwood Hotel and his brothels afresh. What they found was the crowning piece of evidence, or rather, six crowning pieces of evidence.

When the police searched the Maskarada night club owned by the family, they found six young women locked in a single room.

Hearing no one in the club, they had broken a window in an attempt to escape, but were unable to get out and gave up hope until the unexpected arrival of the RS police. The women were from Moldova and Romania; they lost no time in telling the police that they were prisoners and had been forced to work as sex slaves for the family. The club owner, Ilija Gavranovic, a cousin of Milka, was also arrested at the same time. In different operations, Niko Arsenic was arrested for forgery along with other members of the Milakovic gang. Milka and Sasa, the mother and son, had fled the nest. We were later told that as soon as Milorad was arrested a phone call was received by them and they were on their toes and away as quick as lightning. The game was on and the game was up.

The six young women were taken care of by the International Organisation for Migration (IOM) and housed in secret safe houses. They were interviewed at length and gave damning disclosures as to how they were tricked into going to Bosnia where they were forced to work as prostitutes. They described how if they objected or tried not to have sex with customers they would be beaten by the bouncers and guards at the clubs. They all made statements over the next few days, statements that if we could get them to confirm by testifying in court would sink this whole criminal gang. This was a big challenge but a more imminent one was pressing. George Mills phoned me during the evening of the arrests. He was concerned that if this case stayed in the RS, it was possible that public officials on the pay roll of the Milakovic family would find reasons to bail Milakovic, in which case he would flee like his wife and son or, worse still, find reasons to abate the legal proceedings. He told me that people in the Bosnian prosecutor's office shared this concern. He said that Mr Durcevic would sign an order commanding the RS police to deliver the prisoners to Sarajevo for the case to be dealt with at the state court level. However, he was concerned that some senior police officers would not comply with the order and get the case to the court in Prijedor, where he would be bailed or the case dismissed. After all, this is the court where eleven RS police officers were acquitted over the unlawful imprisonment of Fr

Matanovic and his family. It was imperative we get to Banja Luka early the next morning following his arrest and serve Mr Durcevic's order personally.

At 5 am on Friday 9 May, George and I plus another international lawyer from the OHR set off to make sure this case was transferred to Sarajevo. I usually enjoyed the four-hour journey to Banja Luka from Sarajevo, but this time worry and doubt clouded my mind. We travelled through Travnik, the old Ottoman capital of the country, where a castle on a hill guards a pass through the mountains. We then drove higher along the 'Clog Route', a Dutch army main supply route which follows a simply breath-taking ravine, past Jajce, another town with medieval castle, then over the mountains through forests and down into Banja Luka through Cheddar Gorge. This is a beautiful country. We met Jean Pierre and Captain Jean Philippe Plassard in Banja Luka and drove to the RS police headquarters. I was anticipating a fight but not the uphill slog I was to face. We were met by a stony faced Minister of Interior (of the RS). I introduced our delegation and explained we had come to personally serve a notice transferring the Milakovic case to the state court in Sarajevo. The Minister told me that the investigation team had been given all the assets needed, offices, cars and support plus they had carried out a diligent enquiry. He said he wanted the case to be handled within the RS and by the RS prosecutor and for the case to go through the Prijedor court. That was it, nothing more to be said. It was more or less, thanks for coming, don't trouble us again. I thanked the Minister for the diligent work of his police officers, but reiterated the fact that he had been served with an order signed by the state prosecutor, this case had to go to Sarajevo and there was nothing to negotiate. At his right hand, the Minister had with him a very senior RS police officer who I knew, another giant Bosnian man but with a very ugly face. He erupted in anger, banged the table with his huge fist and shouted in the local language that the EUPM doesn't trust his Minister and refused point blank to hand the prisoners over. It was 'the first man who blinks loses' time.

It was not the first time that I had to endure such a tirade and my response was delivered in a style I have perfected over the years. The more abusive and loud my adversary becomes, the calmer and quieter is my response, which causes so much infuriation in my adversary that they lose hold on their reason as logic is overridden by emotion. In a calm and polite voice, I replied that the RS police had carried out an outstandingly thorough investigation (which was true) and as a disciplined organisation they would comply with the order of the state prosecutor; the prisoners must be transferred to the state court, where they were expected at three o clock that afternoon. I reminded them that we came under the authority of the High Representative, Lord Ashdown, who had taken a keen interest in this case. That was it; I could see the Minister's brain working whilst the beefcake sitting beside him glowered at me. The Minister knew that Lord Ashdown as the High Representative had the legal power to sack him. I knew from my conversations with George that Paddy would back us to the hilt. The Minister's face changed; he could see the writing on the wall. He may well have been an honest man who wanted to display that the RS authorities could deal with the case, but George and I knew that dark forces were abroad and we had to get this case away from the Prijedor court. He agreed to transfer all the prisoners immediately to Sarajevo, took the order from the table and passed it to the ugly giant. 'Do it,' he said in Serbian to my smouldering opposite number in the RS Police.

Later that afternoon, George and I were present outside the State Court in Sarajevo when a convoy of vehicles arrived in a sort of Balkan flourish. Heavily armed RS policemen in black combat uniforms and ski masks jumped out of their black Toyota land cruisers and formed a protective ring with carbines similar to Heckler and Koch MP5s. They hauled out four manacled prisoners, amongst whom was Milorad Milakovic, and marched them into the building. I had the satisfaction of noticing that he had the look on his face which said, 'This can't be happening.' The four accused appeared before the judge to face a plethora of charges relating to organised crime, sexual slavery and human trafficking and were all remanded in custody. So that was it, eight hours of driving, big fight with ugly man, four bad people remanded in custody, time to go for a slivovitz. No, not just yet; Mr Durcevic called George and me back into court. He told us that the Governor of Sarajevo prison had phoned him and refused to take the prisoners. The prison was full up; they will have to go back to the RS. No way, I thought. Jean Philippe Plassard was still with me, we jumped into a car with our interpreter and sped off to the Sarajevo prison. Upon our arrival we were shown into the Governor's office but he was not there and had apparently gone home. I told his deputy that we were here on the authority of Lord Ashdown and would wait until he came back. Not much more than five minutes later he returned, with a smiling face. He said there had been a mistake, he had not gone home but had been working hard to find some cells he could free up. We were in luck; four cells had become available! I made a phone call to the court and told Mr Durcevic that our guests' accommodation had been arranged. I did wonder why the prison chief did not want to accept Milakovic and his accomplices. Was it because he had received threats not to accept them so they would be sent back to the RS? If so, who would have made them, the family or officials on his payroll? Perhaps he just didn't want to have one of the most notorious criminals in the country in his care with all the dangers that can attract. Now it was time for a Balkan mixed meat special gut-busting dinner, finished off with a slivovitz or two.

On 20 May 2003, Milorad Milakovic appeared back before the state court. He made an impassioned plea to the court that he was 'happy' on the day that he had received an invitation to appear in the state court of Bosnia and Herzegovina because he was proud of his country. This claim somewhat bemused those listening because he was known to be a Serbian nationalist who had entertained Serb nationalists such as Cetca, the pop star wife of 'Arkan', the Serbian paramilitary and leader of the 'White Wolves' who had wrought havoc in the Balkans, including the Pristina area of Kosovo where I had seen his handiwork close up. The last place Milakovic wanted to be was in Sarajevo. He went on to complain of harassment by the police of the RS who, he said, had deluded the international community by lies which exposed him and his family to unnecessary torture. This led, he said, to the RS police and UN IPTF prosecuting his wife Milka for trafficking, but, he added, the case collapsed because the girls who were then working for her testified to the court that they were treated in a correct and fair manner. He claimed that young women currently employed by his family were happy to work for him and that they had entered the country legally. They had, he claimed, fully co-operated with the visa regime and had submitted themselves to open and honest health checks with the medical authorities. The women were well paid and happy. There is no doubt that some women were content to work for him to try and settle financial problems for themselves and families in the poorer countries they had originated from. He had formed an association of bar owners – in effect his front men – to present a professional face of his organised crime group. Proving our case was looking like an uphill struggle. He let out a tirade against what he saw as other criminals in the RS who had evaded prosecution and the only reason he was being charged was to draw attention away from scandals involving these people, who, he said, were war profiteers and involved in massive tax evasion. He took the trouble of naming some of these people who he believed should be in the court instead of himself. The prosecutor questioned him closely and in detail. It was clear from his statement that he was going to fight this all the way and unless we could produce some of the young women who had been held in sexual slavery by him we were going to struggle.

Thanks to an enormous amount of effort, Madeline Rees, of the Office of the UN High Commission for Human Rights (OHCHR), managed to find countries in Europe which would be willing to give asylum to the six women, in one case also her child, following the raid on the Maskarada night club. The senior politicians in Bosnia were agreeable to issuing visas for the women to enter and leave the country as often as was necessary for the court to take evidence from them, which it did. They were given a special status as protected witnesses and all told similar stories. They related to the court how they had answered advertisements in local papers to work abroad as barmaids, waitresses, or hostesses; Italy was one country mentioned. When they answered the advertisements they were met by a combination of men who the women volunteered to accompany, ostensibly to Italy. The men they met and named were Milorad Milakovic, Sasa Milakovic and Darko Ginjatovic. They usually travelled by bus through Romania or Moldova to Belgrade into Serbia, then either direct into Bosnia or via Montenegro. When they arrived in Bosnia, they were met by bar owners such as Ilija Gavranovic of the Maskarada night club, their passports were taken off them and they were told to work as prostitutes to repay their transportation costs. Refusal would mean a beating. Instrumental in their 'instruction' was Milka and her daughter Sanja, a lawyer, who also provided them with exotic clothing. This was a family business. As a result of the work of the RS police and state prosecutor, assisted by an international prosecutor from the OHR, the four original defendants appeared back before the state court on the 11 and 12 March 2004. Such was the weight of the evidence, including the testimonies given by the protected witnesses, that all four defendants entered pleas of guilty to a variety of charges which revolved around being involved in organised crime, transporting trafficking victims and sexual slavery. Milorad Milakovic was sentenced to nine years imprisonment; Ilija Gavranovic three years imprisonment; Darko Ginjatovic three years six months; and Sanja Milakovic two years imprisonment but suspended for her to perform 200 hours of community work. Milorad's wife Milka and his son Sasa remained at large and were reported to be variously in Russia or Serbia. Niko Arsenic and thirty-one other persons who included family members, bar owners and bouncers were all indicted by the state prosecutor and had to face separate trials.

Between 1996 and 2002, the RS police and then the UN IPTF conducted twenty to thirty raids on the bars owned by this family. The UN, during the period the STOP teams operated, claimed to have carried out 240 raids, closed 142 premises and 'rescued' 265 women throughout the whole country.[10] At least 200 women were used in prostitution by the Milakovic family alone during this time and a number made direct allegations of trafficking against this clan. Despite all this available evidence and several separate investigations, not one prosecution against the main family members was successful. It was not until the main focus was switched from the bars and rescuing victims, to taking out the key players and brains behind the operation, in other words, Milorad Milakovic, that the law enforcement agencies were successful. Furthermore, this was not the only criminal family to be selected as 'targets' by the local police supported by the EUPM. The confidence and ethos of intelligence-led policing grew and more and more successful operations would follow. The local police also established closer links with the law enforcement agencies in surrounding countries such as Romania, Moldova, Croatia and Serbia and the dream of Dr Bob Gravel was finally realised.

I hope it is clear that the investigation, arrest and conviction of major and organised criminals is anything but the work of one heroic policeman acting alone in the aura of his own brilliance. Rather it is a team game, in this case involving the Royal Military Police, the RS Police, the EUPM monitors, the office and involvement of the OHR, the Bosnian prosecutors, international prosecutors, Bosnian politicians, IOM, UNOHCHR, UNICEF, Bosnian local government and department of health officials, the victims themselves and the good people of Prijedor. What was required of me was to be a bit like an orchestra conductor; I had all the right musicians. I just needed them to play all the right notes and necessarily all in the right order.

Chapter Ten
Endings and New Beginnings

I served over two years in Bosnia and Herzegovina and must say I felt that due to the length of time I was there and the people I met and worked with, I was able to leave behind some structures and processes which are still resulting in criminals being arrested as I write ten years later. The 'Tasking and Co-ordinating Group' comprising the chief CID officers from all parts of the country and border service headed by the state prosecutor still work together, share intelligence and coordinate action on national level criminals. I had taken all these CID officers plus Jasna on a trip to the UK in 2003 to visit Scotland Yard and my police force in Dorset. It was very satisfying to see Croat, Serb and Bosnian Muslims all getting along together so well in that common bond that real police officers understand in a special way.

I am also very glad to know that 'Crimestoppers' is still also operating in Bosnia but under its own local name of '*Krimolovci*' (Crime Hunters). Crimestoppers is an American invention which started in New Mexico when a police sergeant encouraged the local people to give information to the police in a murder case where they had previously been reluctant, through fear or intimidation to do so. The anonymity which was guaranteed by the sergeant had the effect of vital information being given which cracked the case. Following this success, Crimestoppers was born and first spread throughout the US and then entered the UK, where it has been responsible for thousands upon thousands of arrests of major criminals. The idea to launch Crimestoppers or a version of it in Bosnia was not because of my own gifted intuition, but once again because I knew some bright people. I had made it my business to meet with the US Department of Justice International Criminal Investigative Training Assistance Programme (ICITAP) team based in Sarajevo. The Americans are involved all over the world in international development, but tend to operate alongside international organisations rather than within them. The Americans at ICITAP were all experienced law enforcement officers and I ran over the organised crime strategy which I was developing for the EUPM with them. I wanted their seal of approval not because they were Americans, but because they were experienced cops.

Tom Harris, a former FBI agent with whom I worked on occasions, noticed that I had not included 'Crimestoppers' in my plan and suggested it would be a good project to introduce. I immediately realised that Tom's idea was going to be a winner. Bosnia suffered from corrupt politicians, corruption in the police and an invasive influence by organised crime. This was one of a number of tools which could be used to unscrew the nuts on this unholy trinity. I got in touch with the Home Office back in London and spoke to Cliff Sharp, a chief inspector on secondment who was my Home Office contact. I explained my proposal to him and requested I be sent out a British police officer to set the scheme up. Within a month or two, I was sent out a detective chief inspector who brought all the Bosnian law enforcement agencies together and within a year *Krimolovci* was up and running. It was entirely due to his skills and the enthusiastic take up of the project by the local police and prosecutors that it became so successful. The obvious threat to the system came from potentially corrupt police officers exposing people who made calls or burying information being given to the police and no action being taken. This was countered by fully engaging EUPM police officers in the system and them being present in the central office where all incoming calls were received. *Krimolovci* is still running ten years later and still resulting in numerous arrests, all thanks to a casual chat with Tom and his American colleagues.

As beautiful as the country is, it is the people, both the locals such as Jasna and Dushanka and the international policemen and women I worked with who have left the greatest impression. I worked with an American policeman who had served two tours with the Marines in Vietnam and came back in his words 'seriously fucked up because all I did was kill people'. Needless to say, when I knew him he had come out of the other side of hell. I worked with a Russian who had fought in Chechnya and who had seen some 'dirty' fighting. Günter was the name of a German policeman who I met shortly after I started with the IPTF. He wore long hair and was of very liberal views, which surprised me because I had the usual inaccurate stereotypical view of Germans. He told me that he never got on with his father who had blown up an American tank in the Second World War just after D Day and was so close to his target that he blew himself up with it as well. Needless to say, he was taken prisoner by the Americans – having just killed a tank crew – and received first aid from them which saved his life. Günter told me that his dad was a Nazi and racist to the end of his life. I regularly worked with a Ukrainian major called Uri, whose wife and son I met several times when we went to the Croatian coast at weekends. He had spent the two years of his national service in a Soviet Union missile silo with his finger literally on the nuclear button. He told us his ballistic missile was pointed at China, but no one really believed him. He was a lovely charming man and his whole family were quite sweet. Amazing to think that if the cold war had turned hot he could have been one half of a two-man team to release his missile and fry millions of British or Americans citizens. This was a generation of men and women whose fathers and mothers had been at war with each other, a generation who could have been at war with each other again had things gone differently. As a boy, I thought that our politicians had learnt the lessons which started in Sarajevo in June 1914 and the calamity which ensued thereafter. But events during the first decade of the twenty-first century undermined that faith.

After I returned from Bosnia, I thought that was it for foreign adventures. Fortune continued to accompany me and I bumped into an old friend of mine, Tony Rogers, who had retired as an assistant chief constable in the South Wales Police. He had set up a company which offered training to the regular police and also offered a service to carry out cold case reviews on certain crimes. As luck would have it, he was in negotiations with a police force in the Midlands concerning a cold case review into the murder of a drug dealer who had been shot dead whilst sat in a barber's chair, 'Chicago style.' I was extremely pleased when he asked me to review the case, which I did over five or six months in 2004. The case was interesting in that the investigation team had placed too much faith in an informant – I had made such mistakes in my earlier career – and perhaps not enough emphasis on some other and actually more obvious lines of enquiry. I duly completed the review with a recommendation from Tony Rogers and myself to re-examine some obvious suspects who had already tried once before to kill the victim. I was about to start looking for work when the phone rang at home.

It was Cliff Sharp, the chief inspector at the Home Office. 'Hello, Tony,' he said. 'We've got a job come up involving helping a foreign police force handle criminal intelligence. Would you be interested?'

'Where is it?' I said, with half an idea I knew the answer.

'Iraq,' he said. 'You would be working out of Baghdad.'

Judith was standing by me when I spoke on the phone, I could see her mind working and it was likely to be 'no way Tony'.

I said, 'Thanks very much, Cliff. It's not so bad up there is it? Let me discuss it with my wife and I'll ring you back.'

He perfectly well understood. I turned to Judith and thought, how do I do this? My ego got the better of me; I felt like James Bond being called out of retirement to save the world. I was fifty-four and had never been in a shooting war. I wasn't getting any younger and it was now or never; besides I might be able to help to get 'our boys' home quicker. My head grew fatter and fatter; I was surprised I could walk through the kitchen door. The problem was that a British contractor had recently been kidnapped and murdered by having his head cut off by a bunch of barbarians and the country appeared to be descending into civil war since George Bush, the American President, had announced 'mission accomplished'. The other problem was that Judith and I were vehemently anti this war as were one million British people who marched in London days before the war started, but the Prime Minister, Tony Blair, who had correctly intervened in Kosovo, in my opinion got this one horribly wrong. Judith was dead against me going but I insisted I would be safe. I said that I would probably remain in the heavily fortified Green Zone and I was sure that it was not as bad as the TV made out. It was in fact far worse. Judith reluctantly agreed and, not two seconds later, I was on the phone to the Home Office before she changed her mind (bad of me I know).

The Home Office required that I should be armed and although I had been a 'silver firearms commander', it was a function which was carried out in the safety of the control room from where operations were commanded at that level. I subsequently underwent an intensive firearms course which was conducted by the West Mercia Police and I learned how to draw and fire a Glock 17 hand gun like a cowboy. I then attended a pre-deployment course and received instructions in avoiding land mines, dealing with the Iraqi police and surviving some of the unpleasant bugs and spiders found in a country with so much desert. All I had to do before I went was to pass a medical examination. No problem I thought, I was pretty fit, ran three miles a day, didn't smoke having given up years before, it was going to be plain sailing. Then there was a snag. My hearing wasn't quite up to scratch, so the lady who examined me said. I couldn't believe it; she said that because I was below the required standard then I had to be considered a failure, it was game over. I told her my hearing was fine and that I had an appointment for an ear syringe, perhaps it was that? She said, 'Oh, in that case, I can carry out the procedure myself,' which she did there and then. She made an appointment for me to return the following morning.

I had bought myself a respite. I returned the next day bright and early but far from bright myself, as I hadn't slept a wink all night. I desperately wanted to go on this mission. I was early and the doctor had a dog. Luckily (yet again) I am also a dog owner and know how people, especially women, dote on their dogs. I went into overdrive telling her how lovely the dog was – which was true, it was a lovely creature. I told her about my own rescue dogs and the sad story of how one of them had been badly ill-treated and how my wife and I had managed to put her life back together again. I then took the hearing test for a second time. I knew my hearing wasn't as good as it should have been. I put the earphones on and listened to a series of bleeps as the test commenced. I quickly guessed that as the sounds decreased and I couldn't hear anything that in fact there were still audible sounds. I did the only thing I could and started guessing when I couldn't hear anything at all. If you've had a hearing test you will know what I mean, the sound gets fainter and fainter and you know there must be something there, otherwise you wouldn't still have the headphones on. But I think the doctor knew I was bluffing.

'I am only going for a year and I will be in an office in the Green Zone, it's not like I'm going to be a front line soldier,' I said. I stroked her dog lovingly and said, 'My ears are buzzing a bit since you syringed them, maybe it's that?'

Whether the doctor was swayed by my love of her dog and my heroic capabilities to rescue other dogs, or more likely because she thought I sounded so pathetic she said, 'Maybe it's because of the syringing, which could cause a temporary slight decrease in your hearing,' she paused and said, 'so I'll pass you.'

I could have kissed her and in my mind punched the air like an ecstatic footballer having scored the winning goal, I was through. I was off to take part in one of the most pointless military campaigns since we went to war with Germany in 1914 because a Bosnian Serb killed an Austrian Archduke and his wife in Sarajevo in June of that year.

looking forward to the helicopter trip from Baghdad International Airport to the Green Zone either, on account of the fact that several weeks before, a Ukrainian helicopter had been shot down flying between the airport to the Green Zone and those who survived the crash were all shot dead by insurgents. The insurgents were former Saddam supporters comprising members of the fedayeen, a paramilitary organisation loyal to the Ba'athist party and myriad other militias and former Iraqi army loyalists. The first thing to learn about Arabic culture is that loyalty to family, tribe and religion are the most consistent and deeply held feelings, loyalty to country comes very much fourth.

The journey out was almost like a civilian scheduled flight, apart from being served the in-flight meal by a hostess in military uniform and all the passengers wearing the same desert fatigues. However, as the aircraft neared Basra, the reality kicked in and we all had to don our kevlar helmets and body armour. The lights were extinguished for the final approach and all I could see was the illuminated reflective strip on the back of soldiers helmets, there was complete silence as everyone was alone with their thoughts – and no doubt prayers – until we touched down, when I could feel the sense of relief throughout. Delivering this number of troops to a combat zone in one aircraft was always a very vulnerable time for the UK military. Whilst the approach path was always swept and guarded by the RAF Regiment, it was nonetheless a time of peak exposure. I got out of the aircraft to be met not just by a wall of heat, but at eight o' clock in the evening, by a sultry humidity which made me feel like I had been locked in a greenhouse in the height of summer for hours. It was appalling and I wondered if I would ever be able to cope with the oppressive climate. Upon landing, I was shocked to find all the soldiers lined up by a carousel just as you see in commercial airports and 200 military rucksacks came tumbling along the conveyor belt. Needless to say, each had a variety of coloured streamers to denote a unique identification. I had an easier job to identify my rucksack which had wheels as is common in civilian life and as I trundled it to my overnight quarters a wheel broke, and I hoped that Fortuna the goddess of good luck, had not

ILLUSTRATIONS

Kosovo
Images 1-9

Bosnia
Images 10-19

Iraq
Images 20-35

Israel/Palestine
Images 36-41

Image of Margaret Hassan reproduced with the kind permission of Care International

Image of Brian Tilley reproduced with the kind permission of Brian's sister, Aileen Tilley

MAPS

1. *Bob Lamburne Mick Clarke - Exhumation in progress. Bob Lamburne left, Mick Clarke on the right.*

2. *Stretcher party - UK Police officers carry the corpse of a murdered Kosovo Albanian to a nearby army lorry for onward transportation to Pristina mortuary.*

3. KFOR sweep - Explosive Ordinance department (EOD) Swedish army engaged in search for explosives with sniffer dog before exhumations commence.

4. Local villagers help in the exhumation process. The British forensic team encouraged the local people to become engaged in the exhumations to help them in the process of dealing with their bereavement.

5. *Women waiting - Mothers wait whilst their men folk help the military and UK civilian police to exhume their loved ones.*

6. *Body in bag - Human remains removed by the UK police team into second body bag due to deteriorated condition.*

7. Clothes show - Clothes were removed from unidentified victims, dried and displayed so that the relatives of the missing could view them and try to identify their loved ones.

8. PM head - The brutal reality of war (crimes). The remains of a man who had been dead and in the ground for over a year.

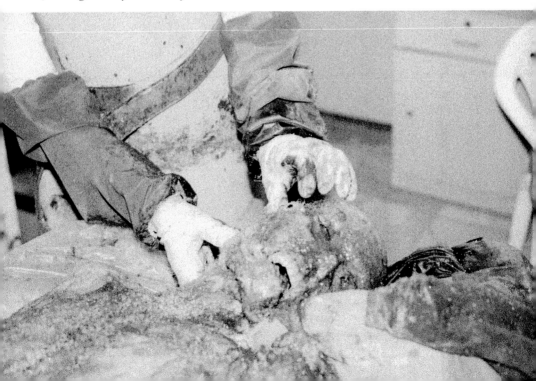

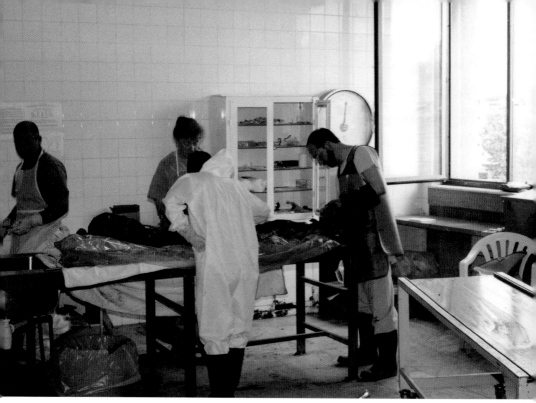

9. *Autopsy Sue Black - An autopsy in progress in the mortuary Pristina. Professor Sue Black centre facing the camera.*

10. *The charm of the Balkans. Taken on the "Clog Route" so called because it was established by the Dutch Army.*

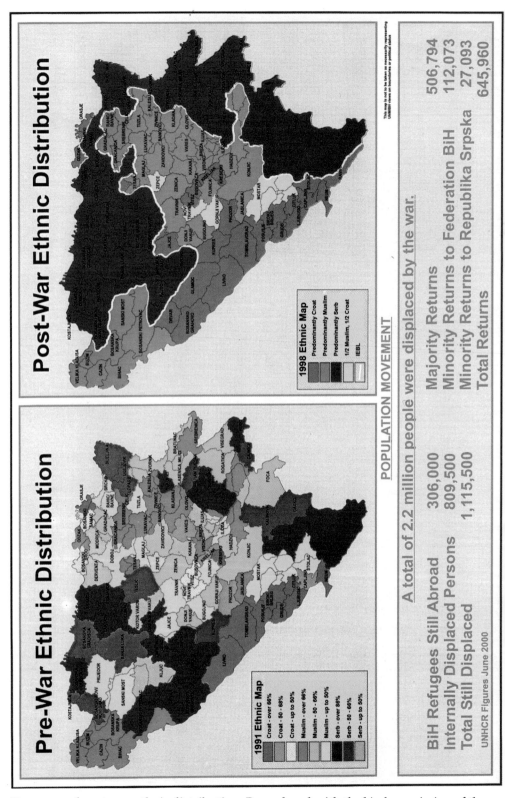

Pre-war and post-war ethnic distribution. Reproduced with the kind permission of the UN.

11. *The lakes around Jayjce central Bosnia.*

12. *SDA was daubed on the walls of these destroyed farms. The Stanka Demokratske Akcije or Party of Democratic Action represented some Bosniak or Muslims in the country. All three sides were guilty of war crimes.*

13. *The rural idyll above Banja Luka.*

14. *Latinski Most, Sarajevo. The site of the assassination of Archduke Franz Ferdinand of Austria and his wife Sophie on 28 June 1914. All western politicians trying to restore peace during the Bosnian civil war were acutely aware that this is where the First World War started.*

15. *The bridge over the river Drina, the boundary between the eastern and western halves of the Roman empire.*

16. *IPTF station commanders meeting Banja Luka. Policemen from the UK; Argentina; Portugal; Austria; Germany; France; Poland; Pakistan; Russia and the Ukraine working together to serve all the people of Bosnia.*

17. *Waseem (Pakistan) station commander Prijador, Tony Nott and Nina my Bosnian Serb P/A at the Kostajnicia signing ceremony.*

18. *Ethnic Cleansing*

19. *Jacques Paul Klein SRSG (centre) with the foreign ministers of Croatia and Bosnia Herzegovina sign the border agreement at Kostajnicia. Note the castle in the background.*

20. *British humour displayed at the accommodation for UK embassy staff. Note the view from the window!*

21. *A view of the accommodation pods for UK Embassy staff in the underground carpark at "The Ocean Cliffs." Whilst the embassy was situated in the Green Zone, the 25 foot high concrete walls did nothing to stop the rain of mortars and rockets which insurgents fired regularly into this "safer" part of the city.*

22. *A room for two. Apart from the air-conditioning being on all night it was tolerably comfortable.*

23. Hummers return from patrol to FOB Shield

24. Taking a break Baghdad 2005.

25. Humvees FOB Shield Iraq 2005. The world's only super power had football fields full of M1 Abrams main battle tanks, but their everyday patrol vehicles were so under armoured that soldiers welded sheets of steel onto the doors and around the top gunner's position to afford better protection. The British army followed suit with the grossly under-armoured snatch Land Rover.

26. These are South African made armoured vehicles used by a private security detail. They have a high wheel base and a boat shape underneath to deflect blast from mines buried in the roads and tracks. They were far better than any comparable vehicles used by the US or British army at the time.

27. *The brave men of the US Army. They were on the road 24/7 for a tour of duty which lasted over a year. Over 4000 were killed in action, thousands more were seriously injured.*

28. *Tony Nott and John Bozicevich as the sandstorm recedes.*

29. *Tony Nott with CRG close protection team FOB Shield 2006.*

30. Downtown Baghdad. A bustling modern city complete with excessive car fumes and equally excessive traffic congestion.

31. View of the river Tigris, from an RAF Puma helicopter. This ancient river runs through the middle of Baghdad.

32. RAF Puma door gunner a long way from Scotland.

33. Margaret Hassan.

34. Brian Tilley.

35. A typical Iraqi police station, half derelict and ill equipped.

Reproduced with kind permission of the UN

UN Office for the Coordination of Humanitarian Affairs
WEST BANK | Effect of closure and permit regime on Palestinian movement
November 2006

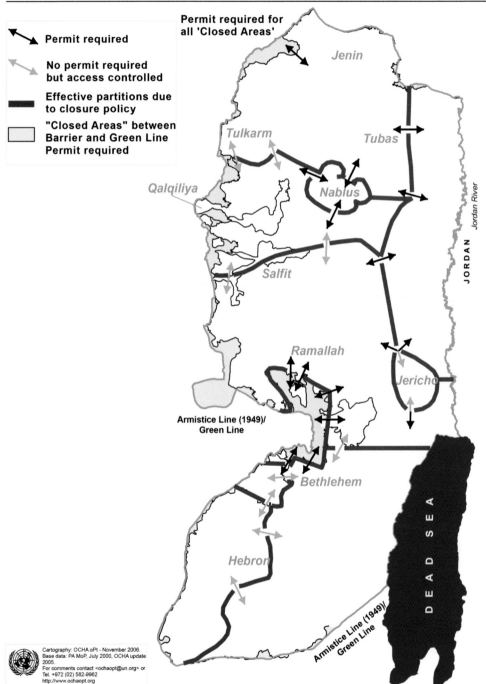

West-Bank Effect of closure and permit regime. Reproduced with kind permission of the UN.

36. *Dove of peace with flak jacket. Seen when entering the Palestinian Authority controlled Bethlehem. Is this a Banksy?*

37. *Separation wall, or fence as the GOI describe it, at the entrance to Bethlehem.*

38. *The wall around Ramallah West Bank: "Control Alt Delete."*

39. *The mountain fortress of Masada overlooking the Dead Sea. 900 Jewish Zealots died here at the end of a siege by the Romans between 78 and 79 AD. They committed suicide rather than surrender. The Roman siege ramp which took two years to construct can be seen on the right of the picture. All Israeli Defence Force recruits take their oath of allegiance at this important site.*

40. *Palestinian prisoners confused and crammed in - Young prisoners held in a Palestinian Authority prison. Cramped and in poor condition the Palestinian guards do their best to make conditions as tolerable for the inmates as their meagre budgets allow.*

41. *Pal security forces - Palestinian Authority anti-terrorist security forces in training.*
The European Union, United states, and other nations help fund the Palestinian
Authority to combat terrorism which is a threat to both themselves and Israelis alike.

chosen to desert me now. A sergeant escorted me to the 'officer's quarters', which resembled a large garden shed in need of some repair. It was dark when I arrived and I had to fumble for my torch in my rucksack which I had stupidly placed three quarters of the way down. I eventually undressed and lay with just underpants on a mattress which appeared to have met a thousand or more sweaty bodies and a pillow which was yellowed with a mixture of sweat and goodness knows what. Needless to say, there was no air conditioning and with the temperature never dropping below about 35 degrees in acute humidity, I barely got a wink of sleep.

The next morning, I was picked up at the accommodation at 6am and I staggered with my over-packed, one-wheel wonky case to the main terminal of what was once a small internal civilian airport. We were then loaded onto a Hercules transport aircraft for an hour's flight to Baghdad. The Hercules is the work horse of the RAF and despite its size, is very agile in flight. Because it is used to carry vehicles and equipment as well as passengers the seating is a sort of sit-in hammock. I wore my body armour and helmet during the flight which for the next year would become a second skin. The passengers, of which there were around ninety, comprised a mixture of British and US soldiers, a number of diplomats and a number of men dressed in civilian clothes but with navy blue body armour and firearms of various descriptions. These latter people were security contractors of mainly British and US nationality and I was surprised at the large number of them. Our flight over the desert was interesting in that I could see small farms and cattle in some isolated parts of what was otherwise all desert. On seeing Baghdad from the air for the first time, I experienced surprise at just how big a city it was. The landing was another excitement in which the pilot descended rapidly in a cork screw pattern to avoid exposure time over the city and dropped this large aircraft with amazing dexterity onto the tarmac. As I walked down the ramp at the back of the aircraft we were greeted by the searing heat of the almost midday sun, but I noticed that mercifully it was a dry heat. Maybe I was going to be able to take this after all.

Baghdad International Airport (BIAP) had been made into a vast American fortification and named 'Camp Victory', such is the American way with words. The operation to invade Iraq a second time in ten years was called 'Operation Iraqi Freedom', following their love of Hollywood. The British name for the campaign was 'Operation TELIC' which I was told interpreted to 'tell everyone leave is cancelled', which is thoroughly British for understatement. I have also been told that it was a name generated by an MOD computer but that sounds even more boring. The next leg of my journey was definitely not boring. After waiting a couple of hours in a huge air conditioned tent with a sea of American service men and women, ebbing and flowing through the tent like the tide, we were called to board our RAF Puma helicopter for the onward journey to the Green Zone. I should explain that the Green Zone is an area in central Baghdad measuring approximately ten square kilometres or just less than four square miles. It contains many key Iraqi government buildings and foreign embassies, including those of the UK and US. The whole area is encompassed by twenty-foot-high concrete T walls, named so because they resemble upside down letter T's. The outside perimeter was guarded by the Iraqi army who have the first interface with people entering this complex. The inner perimeter was guarded by the US army and at each entry and exit point an M1 Abrams main battle tank is stationed in support. It was not unknown for insurgents to send a suicide vehicle-born improvised explosive device (SVBIED) into the outer perimeter and then a second SVBIED shortly thereafter to try to exploit the gap, thus the presence of the tank. The flight by RAF helicopter about which I had had so much trepidation was exactly the opposite of what I had thought. The Puma flew close to the rooftops and cart-wheeled and swooped like a swallow in summer. The door gunner, who had a St Andrews flag on the back of his helmet, waved at the people below, never taking his finger away from the 7.62 mm machine gun he held in a business-like way with his other hand. It was a totally exhilarating experience, even after the aircraft let off flares to confuse ground launched missiles which may have locked on the Puma. We landed at Washington Airport, which is adjacent to the US embassy about ten minutes later. It was here that I started to get the perspective that this was very much a US-led operation and that the resources of the US were truly huge. Black Hawk after Black Hawk were landing and taking off from the helipad every minute; our two Pumas were the only UK aircraft I saw all day.

I was met by a group of men I would get to know and respect and who were identified by their call sign Romeo Three. These were all former soldiers and policemen who worked for a private company called Controlled Risk Group (CRG). These men formed a large private army of bodyguards and sentinels employed by the UK, US and other governments to carry out security work not conducted by the military and there was a lot of work to be done. I was later to notice a distinct difference between the British and US Private Security Details (PSDs). The British tended to conduct themselves in a discreet manner with their SIG carbines tucked under their arms and barrel pointing to the ground; if you blinked you would not have noticed the weapon. The Americans on the other hand, conducted themselves in a more flamboyant manner with their weapon carried at the high porte with the butt on their hip. They often sported goatee beards, were never seen without sunglasses and almost always spoke with a Texas or what sounded like a Louisiana accent. The CRG team who met me were commanded by a thirty-something-year-old former Para and Newcastle Falcons Rugby fan called Robert Swann, but known to everybody as Swannie. He was a fearless, burly man who would, time and again during my tour, get me on US flights when all RAF helicopters were grounded, find ways to get me to locations in Baghdad when all routes seemed blocked and generally protect my life in numerous convoys into the Red Zone with selfless professionalism. He was one of those people who never seemed to be got down by the mayhem all around him and had a wonderful sense of humour; his men adored him. He was killed two years later in northern Iraq when he took a bullet in the neck above the line of his body armour.

I was taken to the UK embassy, which was not far from 'The Assassins Gate' one of the main entrances into the Green Zone.

The embassy was guarded by Ghurkhas who were former UK soldiers and never failed to smile. Outside the main entrance was a Victorian field gun, a testament to battles of old fought in Iraq against the Ottoman Empire. As an American political advisor I worked with later said, 'You Brits have seen this movie before, you know how it ends!' In the inner recesses of the embassy I found my new boss, Colin Smith, a former assistant chief constable in the Hampshire Police, the neighbouring county to Dorset. Colin was a very experienced senior officer, who had served in the Royal Ulster Constabulary during the 'troubles' and then transferred to the Metropolitan Police before settling down in the comparatively peaceful county of Hampshire. He was of generous proportions, had a stubble which passed for a beard but was very much the strategic thinker. He had served the majority of his time as a detective and I would feel confident and at home under his command. I would be his deputy and take over command of the eighty-strong contingent of UK police officers when he was away. He would generally work in Basra where the bulk of the British police were stationed alongside the UK military, training the Iraqi security forces, whilst I worked from Baghdad.

Our primary mission was to help train the Iraqi police to a standard acceptable in a western democracy. The Iraqi Police were the poor relations under Saddam Hussein; the military were his pride and joy, mainly because they were so good at suppressing the many enemies of the Ba'athist party. The Coalition forces, the bulk of which were supplied by the US, had, after the invasion of Iraq in 2003, taken on the responsibility of rebuilding Iraq and turning it from a country led by a dictator into a democracy. The police part of this operation was to work with the Iraqis in training and equipping their police service, which involved a big increase in numbers and roles. My job, other than to help Colin manage the contingent, was to assist a team of American advisors interacting with the Deputy Minister of Interior for police services. In the meantime, after a long day, I was eager to get my head down and I was taken to the complex being used by the UK embassy officials called the Ocean Cliffs!

mortar explosions throughout Baghdad, sometimes far away and sometimes close by, became normal. My experiences during the IRA bombing campaign in London in the early 1970s paled into insignificance.

I was initially allocated a desk at the embassy where I met the very dedicated FCO staff who had a variety of responsibilities and numerous local contacts within the Iraqi upper echelons. Most of them were Arabic speakers. I noticed a number of these high powered political officers had small gaudy plastic tennis rackets (without strings) on their desks. Next to the unbearable heat it was the Iraqi fly which caused the most vexation. They are most unlike their English cousins and would lazily land on your hand which you would wave away. It would then fly off in the most ponderous manner in a wide circle and then flop straight back onto your hand from where it had started its flight. The only recourse for these boffins was to swot the said fly with what was an electronic tennis racket, its blue flash giving some break in the tedium of writing numerous 'e-grams' (cables) back to London.

My first weeks in the mission were taken up with getting to know the other members of the contingent, what they did and sometimes trying to understand why they did it. I was struck by an initial sense of indiscipline, lack of coherent chains of command and a series of private empires built up by different groups of the UK police contingent. One staff officer I noticed did not wear his epaulettes on his shoulders which denote rank and identification. I asked him within a few days of starting work at the British embassy why he did not wear them to be told that it was 'role not rank which were important'. This had been a mantra in the police during the later stages of my service espoused by the young go ahead 'managers' of the time and once again I was out of step. I set up a meeting with Colin Smith to discuss my concerns. He had only recently been deployed to Iraq and agreed with me that something needed to be done to tighten things up and I was 'just the right man to do it'. So once again, I started off in that old familiar role of being the country bumpkin cop telling the big city know-it-all wide boys what to do and how to do it.

Fortunately for me, a number of the older hands in the mission were due to rotate out and as the changeover occurred, so I was able to tighten up discipline and oversight. I had several run-ins with a couple of officers who worked on a group at the US embassy on a joint coalition initiative. This involved them working with personnel who were members of various security services. They did not wear their issued uniforms but wore civilian clothing. I think they thought they were members of MI6 and took on a persona of secretiveness and mystique. There were precious few union jacks on display in Baghdad which was awash with stars and stripes shoulder flashes. I told the officers concerned that they were UK police uniformed officers and I expected to see them in uniform. I got immediate opposition from my proposal being told that it was necessary for them to blend in and it would inhibit them in their work if they wore a police uniform. As their duties involved meeting with other coalition force members in the Green Zone, usually in the US embassy, I was utterly unconvinced by their protestations and insisted that they from now on work in full uniform.

As I was on my way to breakfast in the embassy dining room the following day, I was utterly amazed when I saw one of the officers I had spoken to about to leave the embassy to travel to the US embassy wearing civilian clothes. I asked him why he wasn't in uniform and he replied that he was going to a meeting and didn't think it appropriate. I felt my blood pressure rise to almost bursting point and told him in no uncertain terms to get his uniform on now or get his bags packed and I would get him shipped out as soon as I could get him booked on a military flight. I got no further argument other than a surly grunt. I made a point of telling Colin Smith that morning of the action I had taken over breakfast and I made sure to speak sufficiently loudly so that another contingent member sitting nearby, well known as the 'office gossip', got a good earful of what I was saying. Within hours, the rest of the contingent received the message by way of the bush telegraph. After this incident, things began to slowly improve. It was once again the problem I found in missions, that some officers from various forces do not arrive within their command structures (as do the military) and for a time can be like dogs off leads until they can be identified and pulled in. There existed at this time a lack of selection procedures, but eventually the FCO introduced more rigorous systems, thereby ensuring that the officers they deployed overseas had the skills required and were selected on proven experience and interview.

My next problem was finding a meaningful job to do. I had been given the role by the Foreign Office of advisor to the Minister of Interior, but that role had already been allocated to a senior former FBI officer; the reality on the ground did not match the task I had been assigned. Colin and I sat down and a more realistic role was fleshed out and I was given a desk at the Adnan Palace, one of Saddam Hussein's former residences and told to work with the American-led Civilian Police Assistance Training Team (CPATT). The Adnan Palace is a large, fairly windowless building (I presume to keep out the heat) on the western end of the Green Zone. It was built to resemble a grand stately home but on close inspection reveals a somewhat tacky attempt to 'keep up with the dictators', with an edifice built with no grace, poor joinery and plastic fittings. The ground floor of the palace was awash with a couple of hundred mainly Americans, both military and police personnel, working earnestly on computers and producing myriad power point presentations on everything from organisational charts to syllabuses on traffic law enforcement. My one oasis amongst this sea of advisors was to find Gerry Burke, a former Boston police officer and very experienced Iraqi police advisor who had been there since 2003 and, above all, had a genuine love for the Iraqi people and the job he was doing.

Gerry gave me a run down on the whole show and in the first few weeks I read copious amounts of information about the Iraqi police, their organisational staffing, training and overall responsibilities. The Iraqi police as I mentioned earlier were the poor relations in Saddam's power structures. First came the army, which was more a repressive organisation which had suffered grievously in the Iran-Iraq war. Next came the *fedayeen* which numbered 40,000 to 50,000 men. They were a Saddam loyalist group which reported directly to Saddam, were corrupt and oppressive particularly towards the majority Shia population.

After this came the *mukhabarat* which was the secret intelligence service who spied not only on perceived international enemies but also penetrated and dealt with anti Saddam elements in Iraq. They were considered to be responsible for the attempted assassination of President George H Bush in April 1993. There were also a plethora of other government and tribal groups all with various powers and influence. The impact that tribal leaders had in Iraq as well as other Middle East and Islamic countries cannot be underestimated.

The Iraqi police therefore came a long way after many of these organisations, but were far less tainted by politics. In 2003, the Iraqi Police numbered under 20,000 officers and men. The Coalition wanted to build this into a national police service of 135,000 officers and men which stood at 80,000 when I was there. This number was in my view more than should have been needed for a country the size of Iraq with a population of 37 million. I also use the description 'officers and men'. The Iraqi police were structured along military lines, the officers were educated, but many of the police men and women less so. The whole structure needed building, plus proper pay, human resources, training, policies and procedures and everything else which comes with running such a major public body. The problems facing the coalition were immense but without the powers to dismiss corrupt police personnel, which when I was in the UN in Bosnia we could do, the whole thing needed doing with the co-operation of the Iraqis. The words of T.E. Lawrence of Arabia were frequently quoted by British and American personnel. 'Better to let them do it imperfectly than you do it perfectly, for it is their country and their war and your time is short.' The Iraqi Police Service (IPS) were claimed by one police general I worked closely with, to be losing 250 men and women killed in action each month, with 400 wounded. The police and country was struggling to survive and the whole operation was frequently likened to building a motorway with the traffic still running over it.

I established that one thing missing from the current plans for the Iraqi police was a coherent yet simple local criminal intelligence system. I deliberately used the word criminal intelligence, because to drop the word 'criminal' would conjure up in a post dictatorship Middle Eastern country the spectre of the *mukhabarat* and *fedayeen* whose gathering of intelligence was directed at the ordinary citizen and those of a different political persuasion from Saddam. I felt the best way to proceed was to develop with the IPS a simple system to gather, collate and disseminate information within each police area; to involve all the police regardless of rank; and reboot the whole way crime was investigated at local level. Gerry was supportive of my idea, which he called and is known to American police officers as a 'shoe box card index'.

An important lesson to remember when rebuilding a broken or inadequate organisation is that process is more important than hi-tech hardware. The Americans would have been willing to throw millions of dollars at buying in equipment but it is the process that is vital. For example, gathering criminal intelligence is not just for the chosen few highly-trained specialists. Every police patrol man and woman, parking attendant and other state actors can play a part in gathering intelligence. It can then be sifted, analysed and graded by experienced police officers and then disseminated to all law enforcement officers who need to have the information. Whilst technology helps enormously, it is the involvement of all officers and others in this process which will produce the fertile crop needed to prevent and detect crime. All I needed to do next was to visit some local police stations and see what, if anything, they were doing.

A small number of British personnel worked out of the Adnan Palace and one of those was Brigadier Watters, a studious, thoughtful man whose knowledge of Iraq and the region was immense. I discussed the 'shoe box card index' system with him and he supported my wish to develop this at local level. He was already deeply involved in helping to develop a national criminal intelligence system which dealt with major crime and terrorism and he suggested that I accompany him on a visit to the main police station in Baghdad, where he was to meet the senior police commander for the city the next day. I was delighted at a chance to escape from the Green Zone into the city which was classified as the Red Zone and see for myself the local police at street level. Preparations were made for me to travel with the brigadier in a Land Rover with a small detachment of British soldiers to provide the escort. Everything was going swimmingly until I told the embassy security officer where I was going the next day, when he almost fainted.

'You must be joking,' he said. 'Anywhere you go outside the Green Zone must be reconnoitred, threat assessments made and a full team of three armoured vehicles and nine men provided.' He further said that everything was booked for the next week and I had to put in a request.

I told him I was going with a brigadier in the British army with a full complement of soldiers around me, I didn't consider myself as at the same level as a brigadier so what was the problem, I asked.

I was told that the army take a higher risk threshold than civilians and their vehicles do not have the high level of protection as used by civilians operating out of the embassy. I was dumbfounded. I could not get over the fact that our soldiers face severe risk every day and yet their civilian masters are afforded greater protection in better armoured vehicles for the far fewer trips made by them. This claustrophobic security blanket was to stifle me further as the mission went on, but for now my bid to meet Iraqis in the field was stymied. As a direct result of my frustration and the lack of interaction with the Iraqi police, Brigadier Watters and Gerry Burke made it plain that my place should be working at the Ministry of Interior building in central Baghdad and my escape from the Green Zone would come to fruition in due course. You cannot build a police force while sitting behind a twenty-foot-high concrete wall when all the local police you need to interact with are on the other side of it.

Chapter Thirteen
Margaret Hassan

Whilst I was negotiating my move out from the Green Zone to the US Forward Operating Base (FOB) Shield which was situated close to the Ministry of Interior and the Iraqi Police Academy in central Baghdad, Colin Smith gave me a call and asked me to see him in his office at the embassy; he needed to brief me about a case he wanted me to take on. The task was to act as a link between the Anti-Terrorist Command in the London Metropolitan Police and the Iraqi Police Service in Baghdad, who were engaged in investigating the kidnap and probable murder of Margaret Hassan, a British citizen and humanitarian aid worker in Iraq, which had occurred some months earlier. This is the story.

Margaret Hassan was born in the Republic of Ireland in 1945; her father served in the Irish Guards during the Second World War. When Margaret was four years of age she moved with her family to London, where she grew up with her three sisters and brother. In 1970, Margaret met her future husband, Tahseen Ali Hassan, an Iraqi national who was working as a travel agent at Heathrow airport. They married two years later and Margaret moved out to Iraq, where she worked as an English teacher with the British council.

Following the first Gulf War, the British Council closed down, which was not surprising with Saddam Hussein still in charge and Margaret went through a period of unemployment. In 1992, she started work with a humanitarian aid organisation based in Baghdad called CARE International and soon became immersed in projects involving the provision of food to the poor and needy, the supply of fresh drinking water and sewage disposal. She was also responsible for obtaining financial aid for Iraqi hospitals and in particular the provision of a spinal injuries unit. The financial and trade sanctions imposed on Iraq before Gulf War 2 impacted on the people of Iraq and in particular children who were going hungry. Because Margaret worked so closely with the local people, she saw at first hand the suffering which had been caused. She established a programme for the funding and provision of hot meals to Iraqi school children, who would have otherwise gone without. Margaret devoted herself to the service of the less advantaged people of Iraq and rose steadily to a position where she became the in-country director for CARE International whose head office was in Australia. I was later told personally that she would think nothing of giving her own money to members of her staff who were experiencing financial difficulties; she was without doubt a dedicated, virtuous woman of the highest moral integrity.

Margaret became quite prominent in the world of humanitarian aid workers and was outspoken in her criticism of sanctions imposed on Iraq leading up to the second Gulf War. She was highly critical of American and British foreign policy and delivered a speech to the United Nations in a vain attempt to discourage the use of military force. Margaret lived a busy life which she devoted to the service of the Iraqi people, but this all changed on the morning of Tuesday 19 October 2004. Just after seven that morning, Tahseen waved goodbye to her at the gate of their house in Baghdad as she left for work. She was collected by her driver in a company car and she was also accompanied by a guard. He and the driver were unarmed which was at Margaret's stipulation. Shortly after 7.20am and when the car was a few hundred yards from the CARE office in Hay al Khadra, a car pulled in front of her vehicle and stopped suddenly, then a second car drove up behind her and also stopped so as to block her front and rear. About eight men alighted from the two cars and with extreme aggression fired shots, broke her car windows and beat up her driver and guard. Witnesses said that one, if not two, 9mm pistols were discharged. At least two of the assailants were wearing what looked like Iraqi police uniforms; it was not uncommon in a number of kidnap and mass murder cases for the perpetrators to be wearing police uniforms at that time. Some of the attackers got into Margaret's vehicle and drove away at speed, with Margaret now a prisoner. The whole thing was over in seconds. The driver and guard were left at the scene of the attack and they were taken bleeding and bruised back to the CARE office where the alarm was raised.

Later that day, Al Jazeera broadcast a video of Margaret seated with her hands, possibly tied, behind her back and her identity documents displayed on a table. There was no sound on the video and no demands were made. Tahseen, who had been informed shortly after the kidnap and CARE International then made numerous appeals through the media with the help of local people. Great emphasis was made of all the good work which Margaret had carried out in the last thirty years in Iraq.

The UK government were loath to make public statements for the release of Margaret while standing alongside members of her family, as it was thought this would be seen to be playing into the hands of kidnappers. The UK government's position was firmly not to negotiate with hostage takers or terrorists and maintained that Margaret was Irish. The government of the Republic of Ireland however took a different standpoint and just over a week after her kidnap, Bertie Ahern, the Irish Prime Minister, made a televised appeal for her release standing alongside members of her family. Whilst Margaret held both a UK and Iraqi passports she did not hold an Irish passport; she had always considered herself to be British. The Palestinian Authority also added their voice to the appeals being made, not least because Margaret had worked as an aid worker in Palestine many years before. It was at around the time of Margaret's kidnap that the 1st Battalion the Black Watch (about 850 troops in all) moved north from Basra to Baghdad to back up the US army who were about to commence a major assault on Fallujah.

A second video was broadcast by Al Jazeera on Friday 22 October 2004, in which Margaret was heard to beg for help. She appealed to the British people to ask the Prime Minister, Tony Blair, to take the British troops out of Iraq and not send them to Baghdad, a clear reference to the deployment of the Black Watch. She also said that this was why people like Mr Bigley were taken and she didn't want to die like him. She ended by asking the British people to help her. Mr Ken Bigley, a British contractor, had been kidnapped in Baghdad on 16 September 2004 and decapitated on or about 7 October that same year, less than two weeks before Margaret's kidnap.

The weekend after Margaret's abduction, CARE International suspended its business in Iraq and moved to Amman in Jordan. One consequence of this was that the phones in their offices were not manned and there seemed to be no contingency plans in place to deal with any demands made to CARE from the kidnappers for the release of their in-country senior manager. On the Wednesday following, the 27 October 2004, Al Jazeera broadcast the third video of Margaret in which she asked for the soldiers (Black Watch) not to be sent to Baghdad and for all women prisoners in Iraq to be released. She added that she wanted CARE to cease its operations in Iraq. This either indicated that the kidnapers were unaware that CARE had closed, or that the video had been made before the news had been publically announced.

On Monday 1 November 2004 during the morning, Tahseen received what appeared to be the first call from the kidnappers. A man with a Baghdad accent confirmed that he was speaking to Margaret's husband and then said he would send him a recording from his wife. Tahseen asked the man if he could speak to his wife, but the caller avoided the question and said he would phone back later that day, but he didn't. The following day, Al Jazeera received the fourth video which showed Margaret in a distressed state having a bucket of water thrown over her and being threatened by a man. It is very distressing viewing to see such a good decent woman being treated in this way. The kidnappers were clearly unfeeling thugs.

Tahseen received a further telephone call on Thursday 4

November 2004. He noticed on his telephone display that the number calling was Margaret's mobile phone. The caller, a man, told him that Margaret had admitted working for the British government. Tahseen hotly rejected this claim saying that it could not be true or he would know. The caller said that he wanted to speak to somebody from the UK government and wished to arrange a meeting. Tahseen told him that the UK embassy was not interested and that Margaret was a citizen of both Iraq and Ireland, which he had been instructed to say by the UK embassy. Tahseen suggested that somebody from CARE might wish to speak to him. The caller said he would think about it and call back in a couple of days. After this phone call, Tahseen contacted the UK embassy to report this contact and conversation. He was advised by someone within the embassy to establish from the kidnappers if Margaret was still alive and try to find out if the callers were actually the kidnappers and whether they were criminally or politically motivated. The fact that Margaret's phone was being used to make the calls and that the demands made were overtly political should have made the last two questions unnecessary.

On Sunday 7 November 2004, Tahseen received two further calls from Margaret's mobile phone which were from the same man. The caller asked for the telephone number of the British embassy, but Tahseen told him again that they were not interested. A second call was made shortly after and the caller asked for the telephone number of the head office for CARE in Brussels. The caller said that he hadn't been able to get through to the CARE office in Amman and the Baghdad office had closed. He said that he needed someone to negotiate with and seemed desperate. Tahseen got no further calls from this number. He had to field all these calls himself. No one it appears was with him to listen or record the incoming calls, nor was any attempt made to trace the caller. He did not have anyone with him to provide support; he was left to face all this misery alone.

On Monday 8 November 2004, the US Marine Corps commenced Operation Phantom Fury, the assault upon Fallujah. Over the next five weeks 120 Coalition soldiers (mainly US) and more than 1500 persons identified as insurgents were killed. The precise number of alleged insurgents killed cannot realistically be confirmed. The very next day, a video was broadcast by Al Jazeera in which Margaret explained that she needed to obtain permission from Coalition forces in order to access designated areas to work on water treatment and other humanitarian projects. She was making it clear that if she and her team were in a particular area, the Coalition would need to know where they were. Within twenty-four hours of this being broadcast on Al Jazeera, a further video was viewed which showed the apparent shooting of Margaret in the head from the back. This video was subsequently examined by British forensic experts who believe it probably showed her murder. The killer was wearing a shemagh which covered his whole head, leaving a small slit for the eyes; he was dirty-looking and dressed in trousers and shirt of western fashion. He exuded an air of callousness and incompetence.

Margaret had been kidnapped for a total of twenty-three days or a little over three weeks. During this time, the advice Tahseen had received from the UK embassy and Metropolitan Police was to distance Margaret from the UK government and to emphasise her Iraqi citizenship, stressing that she was Irish, which of course she was not. I was assured that at no time did any member of the UK government or agent thereof enter into any negotiations with any suspected kidnappers. The trail then went cold; Margaret's body was not recovered. Tahseen, together with Margaret's close family of three sisters and brothers were devastated by her callous treatment and murder, as were the huge number of friends and admirers she had. But they wanted answers, a lot of answers.

Chapter Fourteen
Mustafa Mohammad
Salman al Jobouri Kidnapper

In the early hours of the morning of Sunday 1 May 2005, the 3rd United States army Infantry Division (3rd ID) and a unit of the Iraqi army National Guard (ING) were conducting a sweep against insurgents along the banks of the Tigris river. They searched a house in the Zafriniyah area of Baghdad, where members of the ING found identity papers in the name of Margaret Hassan and a sealed letter addressed to Tony Blair. They informed their US army compatriots, who quickly established the importance of the find and arrested the three brothers who lived in these farm buildings who were all of the al Jobouri tribe. An agricultural worker hiding in a nearby field was also arrested. In view of the link to Margaret Hassan, the UK embassy was immediately told and a UK police advisor, Constable Peters, who worked on the Coalition US-led hostage kidnap group was informed. He immediately contacted the Hostage and Crisis Unit in the Metropolitan Police who requested him to attend the scene of the discovery, assist in the search and recover any exhibits in accordance with the strict legal procedures which apply.

Constable Peters was coming to the end of his tour in Iraq, but had built up a large store of knowledge on hostage taking in the country and as a consequence had an extensive list of contacts in the Coalition forces and Iraqi Police Service (IPS). He contacted

Major Abdullah of the IPS Major Crime Unit, with whom he had worked on many previous occasions, who agreed to meet him at the farm house at Zafriniyah. Constable Peters explained his urgent requirement for transport to the scene of the discovery to the embassy security officer and he was given immediate priority. Three armoured vehicles plus a team of six CRG armed body guards took Constable Peters to Zafriniyah where he met the 3rd ID commander. There were almost eighty US and Iraqi soldiers in and around this group of farm buildings located on the outskirts of Baghdad. Also present were three Iraqi men with their hands secured behind their backs and who had been blindfolded. The hooding of suspects is illegal in international law except in certain circumstances. It was the practice in Iraq to cover detainees' heads with hoods because the police and army were worried that these persons could identify them and later murder them. Constable Peters with Major Abdullah questioned the three arrested men regarding possession of the documents found in the name of Margaret Hassan. They all denied any knowledge of knowing about the kidnap, imprisonment and murder of Margaret Hassan, except Mustafa Mohammad Salman al Jobouri. It was in his room that Margaret's property was recovered and he explained that he had been asked to look after it by a friend but claimed he had no part in her kidnapping. Constable Peters then spent the next two hours seizing, photographing and documenting all the property recovered, some of which belonged to Margaret and some to the suspects. He did his best to photograph the farm and outbuildings and then for security reasons everybody needed to leave the scene as such a large static group of coalition soldiers would attract enemy fire. It should be borne in mind that had this seizure been made in the UK, a forensic team would have taken at least two weeks to examine what was a potential site of Margaret's imprisonment and murder and place where so much important evidence was recovered. Constable Peters' work was conducted in a very dangerous environment and no one could have made a better job of it.

The issue of what to do with any prisoners arrested in

connection with the abduction and murder of Margaret had already been considered by the UK embassy and Metropolitan Police after her kidnapping. The decision was that Iraq was a sovereign country, her kidnapping was a criminal offence in Iraq and it was the responsibility of the Iraqis to investigate it and deal with any persons arrested. Thus it was that the persons arrested were eventually handed into the custody of the IPS. This did not take place immediately as there was a fear that persons arrested by the Coalition could end up being tortured by the Iraqis, so their transfer to the IPS was managed with this in mind and guarantees were obtained. This formal transfer of arrested persons from a US-controlled detention facility into Iraqi custody took several days to accomplish.

The property seized from the farm house included CARE identity cards in Margaret's name, personal possessions in a handbag later identified as hers and a sealed letter addressed to Tony Blair. This comprised a note which she had written containing the words she used in the second video asking that British troops be sent home and not be sent to Baghdad. A set of registration plates were also recovered which had been removed from the vehicle in which she had been travelling when she was abducted. Some personal papers of Mustafa al Jobouri were also seized; these included a permit to possess a 9mm Browning automatic pistol indefinitely and a Ministry of Foreign Affairs identity card. Most poignant of all was a small picture card of the Virgin Mary, of the type which often mark places in prayer books or bibles. Margaret was a devout Roman Catholic who attended mass in Baghdad regularly.

Shortly after the arrest of the four suspects, Constable Peters rotated out of the mission having completed his one-year deployment, so it fell to me to carry on where he left off. To confirm my exact role, this is how I was instructed to proceed. The abduction and murder of Margaret took place in Iraq, which had the jurisdiction and a working criminal justice system to deal with the crimes committed. The investigation was conducted by the IPS; the Metropolitan Police would assist in any way in which they could and had already put their considerable forensic capabilities at the disposal of the Iraqis. All they had to do was ask. The Metropolitan Police would monitor the investigation but their officers did not have the permission of the commissioner of the Metropolitan Police to travel outside the Green Zone. I was a retired police officer working on a one-year contract with the FCO. As a result, I could travel in the Red Zone under the terms and conditions which the embassy security officer considered appropriate. These were the same for all FCO staff. The Ministry of Interior is situated in down-town Baghdad and several miles from the Green Zone. It fell to me therefore to be the link man between the IPS investigation team led by General Raad, the embassy and the Metropolitan Police.

Having been assigned this case, my first job was to sweep up all available papers and records of what had happened and consume the data. Next was to fix up a meeting with General Raad and his team, which I did within a few days. It was also good practice for me to buddy up with another officer as two heads are better than one on a case like this which needed constant attention. Should one of us be elsewhere, there would always be another officer in theatre. I was very fortunate that Colin assigned me Josephine or Jo Jones, a tough intelligent police inspector from Hampshire with particular knowledge of matters involving terrorism. Jo, a tall, lean woman with long dark hair, soon got busy organising the paperwork and finding all the detailed material we needed.

What we both discovered very quickly was that there had been an insufficient central point of contact between the Metropolitan Police, the FCO and the investigating Iraqi police team. The Iraq war was deeply unpopular in the UK. The Labour government led by Tony Blair with his Foreign Secretary Jack Straw were both under considerable pressure every single day from their many critics, both in politics and the media. As soon as a soldier was killed or an incident such as the abduction of Margaret occurred, opponents of the war would speak out at home both decrying the government and seeking political advantage. The Foreign Secretary was also under intense pressure from Margaret's sisters and brother to come up with answers; they were far from happy with the government's handling of the case. However, the Foreign Secretary and the FCO stuck rigidly to the government's policy of not negotiating with terrorists. This must have caused agony for the family as it appeared their sister had been abandoned, with Tahseen left to deal with phone calls from the kidnappers; it is no wonder the Irish government tried to do what little they could. Thus, this pressure transferred from the elected politicians to the FCO who always had to find answers to assuage these critics. The result was that various FCO officers would get questions to the IPS demanding answers to their issues, whilst at the same time the Metropolitan Police were trying to answer the same questions to the FCO and in turn raising the same issues with the IPS. Therefore, with the ambassador's direction and authority, I became the single point of contact with the IPS and so was able to streamline the process and saved the IPS the need to run around to different bodies answering the same questions.

Later that same month I drove out to meet General Hussein AK, who was involved in the investigation and who worked in the MOI. There had been some internal Iraqi police politics and General Hussein AK was becoming engaged in the investigation alongside General Raad. I needed a full update on the IPS interviews with the suspects to establish what they had said under questioning.

The drive to the MOI was what was now becoming the standard roller coaster ride through the city. The convoy of three armoured four-wheel drive vehicles would wait at the exit to the Green Zone until the team leader got the words 'good to go'. I travelled in the middle vehicle, the other two front and rear each with at least two CRG guards inside. At every junction, the lead car would block any side roads and we would go forward to be replaced by leap frogging protection vehicles as we proceeded. I remember many times passing the 'two towers internet cafe' with crude paintings of the burning two New York skyscrapers, just to remind you of the attitude of some Iraqis to the murder of 3,000 innocent working men and women. After about twenty minutes, we arrived at the Ministry of Interior. Coalition Convoys were regularly hit by IED's along this route; after all, there were only three or four routes in and out of this central complex and for the insurgents it was like shooting fish in a barrel.

General Hussein AK was an elegant, highly-educated man from Northern Iraq. He had a shock of grey hair and the almost obligatory moustache. I was surprised to see grey hair because in the days of Saddam Hussein, all his chief officers and acolytes were sure to dye their hair black to avoid being thought of as old. He was a proud Kurd with his own Peshmerga bodyguard. The general told me that there was no evidence that the two brothers of Mustafa al Jobouri could be linked to the abduction and murder of Margaret, despite the fact that one had been a major in the intelligence service and was a member of the 'Saddam Association' which meant he had been personally commended by Saddam Hussein on three occasions. He could also speak excellent English. Less was known about the second brother but all three appeared to be what was termed 'Former Regime Elements' (FRE). Mustafa had been questioned by the IPS and by General Hussein AK himself. As a result of these interviews and enquiries by the IPS, a picture was emerging of the people who had been involved in the abduction and murder of Margaret. The names of two other men in particular had been obtained from different sources and a third man's name was given who was suspected to have helped bury Margaret's body in a piece of rough ground where non-Muslims were buried. The precise location of the burial plot was unknown but the area where she was buried was locally called the black hill. It was within an area with a high concentration of insurgent activity and a very dangerous area of Baghdad. I later spoke to a US army colonel about the prospect of carrying out exhumations in this area but he considered that it was far too dangerous for Coalition troops to risk being killed or injured by their exposure for many hours in this hot spot in order to recover a dead body. 'I'm not losing any of my men just to guard a hole,' he said. I had to agree that it was not worth losing lives to recover Margaret's body, as did Tahseen, who I spoke to later.

I updated the Metropolitan Police and the embassy about the latest developments of the investigation. The greatest concern expressed was about the conduct of the interviews and whether they were being conducted in accordance with full compliance with human rights legislation. To the best of my knowledge they had been. There was a desire for the suspect, Mustafa, to be interviewed by the British police which would confirm and qualify whether what I was being told was accurate and that any admissions had not been obtained under torture. Any interview would have to take place in the Ministry of Interior, to which the Metropolitan Police could not travel. It therefore fell to Jo Jones and I to carry out an interview with Mustafa, which I decided should be on tape and in accordance with standard police procedures as in the UK. It was also decided by the ambassador, Sir William Patey, a shrewd, blunt-spoken Scot and an accomplished Arabist, that I sit outside the IP investigation so that the UK would not be involved in a process that could lead to the death penalty.

Jo and I drove to the MOI in early July. It was 45 degrees and we were wearing full body armour and helmets, plus we were armed ourselves. We were in the usual three vehicle armoured convoy with about eight or more CRG bodyguards. Due to our security regulations, we could not take the lift and had to walk up over half a dozen floors in a building with no air conditioning and full of tobacco smoke. Almost all Iraqis smoke and the no smoking policy in public buildings fashion hadn't yet hit Iraq. The Americans, who acted under less stringent security conditions, tended to use the lift and customarily tipped the lift operator with 9mm bullets, which were good currency. Each floor of the MOI building was like its own separate fiefdom. The entrance to each level was guarded by the units which worked there, who checked passes and searched visitors. Needless to say, Coalition forces were not searched. On arrival we were shown to a large office at one end of the building, where I met Major Abdullah and his partner, Captain Amir. I worked with them many times after this and can only describe them as the 'Starsky and Hutch' of the IPS, a portrayal they both liked. They brought me up to date with the latest news of the investigation and I explained how Jo and I would proceed.

The prisoner, Mustafa al Jobouri, was then brought in blindfolded and handcuffed. I asked for his blindfold to be removed, which it was. CRG close protection guards were stationed inside the room on the door and along the floors of the building, such was the threat to rescue him. For the next three hours, I questioned him about the handbag and personnel effects belonging to Margaret Hassan which were found on a wardrobe in his bedroom. He said that he had been given them by a friend to look after but he denied knowing anything about Margaret's kidnapping and murder. I questioned him more closely about the persons who had been in possession of her property and asked him to repeat to me what he had told the Iraqi police. He claimed that anything he said to them was because he had been tortured and that he was an innocent student. I reiterated the replies he had given to Major Abdullah and Constable Peters when he had been arrested at his home on 1 May, which corresponded with what he had told the IPS. Those answers had not been given under duress and were also witnessed by members of the US army who were all around at this time. He sulkily admitted some of the answers he gave were true, but insisted he was not responsible for her kidnapping and murder. He went on to explain that he was an engineering student at the al Nahrain University in Baghdad and whilst opposed to the invasion of his country, he believed it should be opposed by peaceful means. However, when I showed him his identity card for the Ministry of Foreign Affairs, he reluctantly admitted he worked there but minimised his role. It was suspected he was part of a unit at the ministry which carried out surveillance on foreigners visiting Iraq. I asked him if he owned a gun and he replied only a shotgun. I showed him a weapons permit with no expiry date for a 9mm Browning semi-automatic pistol with his name and photograph on it and again he reluctantly admitted owning such a weapon. He would only admit the truth when I could put something under his nose to show he was lying. I was only halfway through the interview and due to the hour had to break off until the next day when I would return to continue the questioning. As we drew to a close, a huge explosion occurred as a SVBIED exploded at the outer perimeter of the MOI and the whole building shook; a number of IPS guards were killed. The MOI was one of the most dangerous and frequently targeted buildings in Iraq and I experienced several attacks on the building and surrounding complex during my tour.

Our return to the Green Zone was made more eventful than usual as the vehicle I was travelling in tore its tyre on a kerb when the driver was attempting to cross a central reservation due to a traffic jam we were heading into. We drove a little distance on the flat tyre before stopping for a wheel change similar to those seen on formula one racing, except in this case the pit crew were surrounded by heavily armed men guarding them and all traffic was stopped and kept well back away from us. The fact that where we stopped was overlooked by what appeared to be a run-down housing estate with very poor inhabitants who suddenly became very interested in proceedings, turned an inconvenience into a bit of a worry. In just over three minutes, the wheel was changed, everybody climbed back into their vehicles and we were off again on a circular tour of the city to avoid stopping in the heavy traffic. We were late back to the Green Zone and should have been home earlier. And we had to do the same thing all over again the next day.

Thursday 7 July 2005 started out hot and sunny as usual and after the usual tense journey to the MOI we met General Hussein AK. We discussed the previous day's interview of Mustafa al Jobouri and the ongoing operations by the IPS to trace the rest of the kidnap gang. As I walked to the interrogation room, I noticed a number of prisoners in a holding area in a restricted part of the MOI, all of them wearing blindfolds. Mustafa al Jobouri was picked out from amongst them and brought through to an office for further questioning. I started by asking him about his claims of being tortured by the Iraqi police. Where and when had it happened, I inquired, and by whom? He could not provide any detail to precise questions other than to make a broad claim of torture. I asked him to show me the injuries he had received but he was unable to, claiming they left no marks and that he had been subject to electric shock treatment. I asked to see where any electrical wiring had been attached but he was unable to show any burn marks. He then adopted the same sulky arrogance he had displayed previously. I then went through a series of questions with him on tape as I had the day before and went back over certain explanations he had made. The interview lasted an hour and a half and I managed to obtain from him similar answers to those he had given to the IP and therefore negate his claims of torture. I cannot reveal the full content of these interviews as this investigation remains live and suspects remain at liberty, so any disclosures could prejudice ongoing enquiries. Equally, if I had access to suspects' names that have not been mentioned in the media or other open source material, I cannot give them here.

My return to the Green Zone was without the drama of a pit stop opposite an impoverished council estate, but this time we had difficulties getting through the checkpoint into the Green Zone. Traffic approaching the Green Zone was funnelled into single file lanes with Jersey barriers either side. These are concrete walls about three feet high and once you are in the entry lane you have to wait behind the convoy in front. The vehicles ahead of us had been delayed because one of the passengers did not have the correct paperwork. The usual pattern of SVBIED attacks on the Green Zone were launched by suicide bombers waiting in side streets just before the separation lanes, who would then drive out behind a convoy as it arrived and then detonate their bomb as the target convoy started to move through the checkpoint. It must have taken ten minutes to sort out this delay and I was anxiously looking out of our rear window for what seemed like an hour before we at last moved through the checkpoint and back home again. That evening I debriefed Colin in the 'whine bar' (a small plush bar at the embassy with red leather chesterfields and arm chairs), where Colin got so much whinging from a few officers not happy with their lot. Unfortunately, the embassy was full of the news from London where four suicide bombers had struck, killing fifty-five people on the Tubes and a bus. Baghdad had come to London.

Chapter Fifteen
Loose Ends

As the investigation gathered pace more clues were uncovered, which led in turn to even more lines of enquiry. But before racing ahead, it is important in any investigation to take stock of where you are and 'clear the ground under your feet', as it states in the 'murder manual', the bible for senior investigating officers. There were misgivings about Margaret's driver, who was believed to be linked to one of Saddam's intelligence agencies. Suggestions were made from within the FCO and from some people linked to Margaret that he could have been involved in her kidnapping. Suggestions made like this caused pressure on the Iraqi Police to arrest him, as they wanted to be seen to be doing everything properly.

Therefore, against the better wishes of General Raad, the driver was arrested and interrogated. Raad was conscious that his investigation was being scrutinised by the British and he wanted to demonstrate that he was doing everything to keep them happy. By utter chance, I was in the MOI one August day on other business and thought I'd pop in and see Major Abdullah as my other meeting had finished earlier than expected. I knocked on his office door and walked straight in to find General Raad in the process of questioning a man who was cowering under a stream of what appeared to be robust questioning. Major Abdullah was also there and he explained that the suspect was Margaret's driver; the general was asking him why had he run away and not defended her. I could tell by the tone of his voice that he was telling him in no uncertain terms that he was less than a man and should be ashamed of himself. The suspect was quivering under this verbal barrage and whilst clearly not subject to physical abuse, seemed to be under a lot of strain. I thought it best to remain throughout and whilst possibly exceeding my brief, common sense dictated that my presence was likely to ensure some sort of fairness. Major Abdullah translated for me as the interview proceeded and Raad appeared pleased with his forthright approach, which he probably felt was up to what we British expected. I doubt he fully grasped the type of liberal pluralist society I came from. After his questioning of the suspect who hobbled off, feet shackled, back to prison, I went over the evidence with him. I thanked him for his enthusiasm and effort in following up concerns expressed by the British, but I wanted to know what evidence existed or even suspicion that this suspect was in any way involved with Margaret's kidnap. There was in fact none; he had been arrested to assuage British concerns.

To ensure that all angles were covered, I offered to interview the driver myself, which Jo and I did a few days later. He co-operated fully and answered all questions; we found nothing to implicate him in Margaret's abduction. After a whole month and after much encouragement from myself that there would be no criticism from the UK government, the driver was released. In Dorset, we would have turned this around in less than twenty-four hours, but I was not in Dorset.

Another loose end and a very important one concerned Margaret's husband. A witness statement had been obtained from Tahseen shortly after her kidnapping, but it was missing some detail and needed to be retaken. I met with Tahseen a number of times during the twelve months I was in Iraq. He was a most elegant man, tall and slim with thick grey hair and moustache. He had a noble bearing and spoke with a quiet cultured voice; he reminded me of the famous Egyptian actor Omar Sharif. I introduced myself to Tahseen and updated him with everything the IPS had told me and explained my role as a link man in the case between the IPS and Metropolitan Police. Tahseen told me afresh everything he could about Margaret's kidnap and the subsequent telephone calls he had received from a man who claimed to be involved in her abduction. The precise details of what had been said were incorporated into a new statement as these particulars had not been fully covered in his earlier statement.

Tahseen also told me that about two or three weeks after his wife's kidnapping he had received a call at home from a man who gave the name Abu Mustafa and was speaking on behalf of Margaret's kidnappers. This man proposed a meeting with Tahseen and told him to wait on a particular street corner in the Khadun area of Baghdad at two thirty the following afternoon. Tahseen told me that he contacted the local police, who instructed him to keep the appointment and they said they would put plain clothes police in the area to monitor any meeting. He kept the appointment and waited for about three quarters of an hour on the street corner, but no approaches were made to him. The local police then came out of cover from nearby buildings and told Tahseen that there had been three or four cars cruising around the area. They thought the cars contained members of the kidnap gang who they believed were intent on kidnapping him. They did not explain why they thought this. He was also aware that somewhere in the background, a man of Western origin, but not British, was organising the surveillance operation. He could only remember a part of his name, but it would prove to be enough. Tahseen then went home and the next day he received a phone call from the same man who had called the day before, Abu Mustafa. He said, 'Why did you bring the police with you?' and then hung up. Tahseen never heard from this man again.

It cannot be proved conclusively that this meeting had been arranged by the men who had kidnapped Margaret but neither should it be discounted. This abortive meeting took place two or three weeks after Margaret's abduction according to what Tahseen had said. The suspected murder of Margaret took place not more than twenty-three days after her abduction. I tried over many months to find out who knew what about this failed operation. The Metropolitan Police told me that they were unaware of any such activity, as did the UK embassy. I spoke to Major Abdullah and General Hussein AK and they also said they were unaware of any such action taken by the IPS. I made it my business to hunt down from a variety of sources every file and scrap of information about this case that I could. It took me months of searching, but in an innocuous file reserved for routine administration, I found the name and details of the man Tahseen had vaguely remembered. The correspondence I found linked him to the case in the relevant time period. Despite repeated attempts, I could never get hold of the individual concerned; he returned none of my calls and resided in another Middle East country. Whoever was responsible or involved in this attempt to monitor Tahseen's meeting with the suspected kidnappers remains an unanswered question. The big flaw it revealed is that nobody had control of the overall investigation, certainly not the Metropolitan Police, nor the embassy. There appeared to be no one person in absolute command on the British side with the relevant skills.

Chapter Sixteen
Sheikh Hussein

Despite this brick wall of mystery, things were moving in other areas. General Hussein AK told me that as a result of enquiries by the Iraqi Police, a link had been made to a man known as Sheikh Hussein Ahmad Salman al Zawbai (or Zubayi). He was believed to be a hard line Sunni and a key member of the 1920 Revolution Brigade. This was a known insurgent group whose name had origins back to the 1920s and resistance to the Colonial power in Iraq at that time, namely Great Britain. He was also known to be an Imam at the Mustafa Mosque located in the refugee camp for citizens of Fallujah displaced during the recent fighting. This camp was situated within the al Nahrain University in Baghdad, which specialises in engineering degree courses and where Mustafa al Jobouri said he was a student. Sheikh Hussein was such a respected figure by the Director of the University, Khalid Ahmad Judi, that he was authorised to appoint the guards around the university complex. The IP tried on several occasions to arrest Sheikh Hussein in order to question him concerning his involvement in Margaret's kidnapping but failed every time. They wanted to carry out the arrest when he and his wife, Dr Baan Khaldoon Siddeeq al Rawi, and other persons believed to be involved with Margaret's kidnap, could all be housed and taken at the same time. They never got their ducks in a row.

On 5 January 2005, Florence Aubenas, a Belgian journalist working for a French newspaper, was kidnapped. She had visited

Sheikh Hussein at the Mustafa Mosque in the university grounds with the intention of speaking to him about the humanitarian impact on the residents of Fallujah. After having spoken to him, she went to interview some of the refugees from Fallujah but was met with hostility. The situation was turning ugly and she decided to leave the compound quickly. As she tried to leave the compound, armed men confronted her and both she and her interpreter were taken captive. They were held until June 2005 when they were released, reportedly after the payment of a ransom of $10 million. She later stated that she was spoken to by an Iraqi woman who was referred to by her other captors as 'Doctor,' and this woman could speak French.

On 4 February 2005, Giuliana Sgrena, an Italian journalist, visited Sheikh Hussein at the Mustafa Mosque where he warmly welcomed her. She also wanted to interview refugees from Fallujah which she attempted to do and was met with the same hostile response as her fellow Belgian journalist. She cut short her visit and as she left the university complex, which had become noticeably short of guards, a group of men in two cars blocked her exit, shots were fired and she was taken captive. On 4 March 2005, she was released from captivity into the custody of two men from the Italian security services. She was driven to Baghdad International airport but as she approached the airport US troops called upon her vehicle to stop and when it failed to do so shot into the vehicle wounding her and killing one of the intelligence officers travelling with her. The US army claimed that the vehicle was travelling at high speed and had failed to stop when challenged. They initially fired warning shots and then shot at the engine block. Ms Sgrena claimed that the vehicle was being driven within the speed limit and no attempt to stop it was made before it was fired upon. It was reputed that a $6 million ransom was paid by the Italian government for her release.

Margaret Hassan had been kidnapped on 19 October 2004 from the Karrada area of Baghdad, which is a matter of a few streets away from the al Nahrain University. The abduction of three western women, two of whom made appeals on video for their national troops to be withdrawn from Iraq and kidnapped from within the same area and over a time span from mid-October 2004 to early February 2005 suggests a very striking pattern. Efforts to trace Sheikh Hussein were intensified but he slipped the net the IP had been drawing around him. The IP were under considerable pressure at this time with the insurgency spiralling and told me that several operations had gone wrong. They had received information that Sheikh Hussein had skipped the country to live in Jordan. I felt very impotent not being able to take a more commanding role. I had once had it in my power to orchestrate surveillance, run operations and 'call the strike' on abundant numbers of serious target criminals. Now I had no authority and could only monitor and offer advice; it was all very frustrating.

I suggested that we needed to go to Jordan and follow his trail and make the arrest with the Jordanian police ourselves. The Iraqis felt that their own arrangements to visit a foreign country and make enquiries would be slowed down by protocols. They suggested that it would be quicker if I went to Jordan and liaised with the Jordanian police with an Iraqi officer in company. I agreed and liaised with the embassy and the Metropolitan Police and got the go ahead. I then worked with the IP to obtain the necessary letters of introduction to the Jordanian authorities from the Investigating Judge (this is the Napoleonic system where a judge is the lead investigator). Formal arrangements with the Jordanian police could not be made until they received instructions from their own Minister of Interior, which depended on a letter from the Iraqi counterpart. I was able to set the whole thing in motion, however, through Interpol and therefore the Jordanian police were just waiting for the written permission to cooperate. I had every assistance and support from the UK embassies in Iraq and Jordan, or so I thought and an e mail was sent over a week before I arrived setting out our intentions. General Raad and Captain Amir were to accompany me on the mission and we were in possession of an international arrest warrant for Sheikh Hussein obtained through the Iraqi judge. I had made all the efforts to let all the parties know that we would be flying out of Iraq on 25 October 2005 and I wanted to hit the ground running.

On the day of our departure, General Raad, Captain Amir and I were required to meet with the Minister of Interior, Baqir Jabr, at the Adnan Palace in the Green Zone and get his formal blessing, plus the all-important letter from him to the Jordanian Minister of Interior. I had tried to get General Raad to arrange this meeting well before we left, but he was unable to despite my repeated nagging and growing frustration with the speed at which things operated in Iraq. The Minister had made a point of ordering the general to be in his office at twelve noon that day to receive the letter, which I thought was leaving it late but that was the arrangement. We made it in good time for our appointment and our helicopter out of the Green Zone was at 1.20pm, the helipad (LZ Washington) being only fifteen minutes away. The Minister's suite of opulent offices was on the first floor in the Palace, behind a series of lattice wooden screens. We were met by two well-dressed young Iraqi men in expensive suits who were the Minister's assistants and who, General Raad told me, were related to the Minister. This is not uncommon in Iraq, as most of the elite employ their families around them. General Raad explained that our visit was for a twelve noon appointment and we had come to collect an important letter from the Minister. Both men looked us over in an arrogant and disdainful way, at me in particular, as if I was something unpleasant stuck on the underneath of his shoe. One of the assistants made some kind of pretence of examining my passport and identity cards. We were then kept waiting whilst the two aides wafted in and out of the Minister's office, whose voice I could clearly hear. Several times I approached the two aides and requested that we have one minute of the Minister's time as our departure was becoming imminent. The response was more cool looks from our hosts, one of whom seemed to be oblivious to us and when talking on the phone convulsed into fits of laughter so pronounced I thought he was going to choke. Finally, at one o clock, an hour and twenty minutes after our arrival, I told the two flunkies that we were going. Their attitude changed suddenly and one of them said the

Minister was nearly ready. Well, it was too late, we were off without the all-important letter of introduction. As I walked out of the Adnan Palace, a western man approached me in civilian dress and started asking me about where I was going in Jordan; he had a pronounced American accent. He started to want to talk about the case and Sheikh Hussein as he was also interested in him; he dropped the name of a UK policeman he said he worked with. I told him to contact me when I returned to Baghdad, but he never did and he melted back into the shadows. Who he was I don't know; when I later asked the policeman whose name he mentioned, he didn't know him either.

We then hurried at breakneck speed to get our helicopter to Baghdad International Airport to get our plane to Jordan, but when we arrived at BIAP we were told the flight had been cancelled due to security reasons and we had to wait until the next day. It transpired that one of Saddam Hussein's lawyers had been killed during his trial and reprisals were expected from his supporters. 'Hurry up and wait' is a phrase military personnel know well. I found the CRG guards who had a permanent post at Camp Victory, which is the military base around the airport, but I also had two Iraqis with me and I didn't want them wandering off, especially as I was responsible for them inside the perimeter. Fortunately, a very pleasant and attractive young lady and officer in the USAF came to my rescue. She managed to show me a small part of the base where the new Iraqi air force was setting up. We found two Iraqi air force officers who took General Raad and Captain Amir into their company and within half an hour they were all like long-lost brothers. I then went back to the CRG tent and spent the rest of the day wandering around a small part of Camp Victory killing time. I was amused to watch some American soldiers running through a patch of sand and then taking cover behind some crates pointing their rifles at nothing in particular. Another of their chums was filming their antics on a small video recorder and was careful not to include in the view the thousands of tents that surrounded us. Good stuff to show the girlfriends I guess, of active service in eye rack!

We arrived in Jordan the next day and took a taxi to the British embassy where I had arranged to meet a mid-ranking political officer. I wanted to present my credentials and confirm the times and locations of our visit to the Jordanian police, who would assist us in our search of various addresses where it was suspected that Sheikh Hussein was living. The embassy official I saw was apologetic and admitted they had only just read the email which had been sent from the Baghdad embassy eight days earlier. I was flabbergasted, as I was expecting to get this thing moving straight away, but after some shuffling of papers they promised an appointment would be made for the following day. The lack of a letter from Minister Jabr helped to compound the mess even more. I went back to our hotel, apologised to General Raad and Captain Amir and said, 'Don't worry, the embassy are fixing it up for tomorrow.' It was not until two days later that we got to see the Minister and eventually the Jordanian Special Branch, to track down our man. I expected to work until we dropped rather like we would have done in Dorset, but it was Ramadan and everything stopped at 3.30pm. It wasn't all frustration however and on a further visit to the UK embassy, there waiting for me was my old friend Mick Ashton, the solid strong Yorkshireman and my deputy in Bosnia. He was engaged in training the Iraqi police in Jordan and had heard I would be visiting. We enjoyed a good bowl of tobacco soaked in rose petals in a shisha (hubbly-bubbly) pipe in Amman that evening. For the next several days, together with the Jordanian police, Amir and I searched various addresses in Amman. There was no trace of Sheikh Hussein in any of the places where he was supposed to be. Amir was able to make some additional enquiries locally and it appeared he had been in the places we visited but had disappeared long before our arrival. The information was stale and I got the distinct impression that somebody else had been to each address we visited before us, I was a small player in a big game. At least when we left Jordan a week later, we were able to provide the Jordanian Special Branch with photographs of Sheikh Hussein and other assorted intelligence material plus an international arrest warrant.

In December 2005, I met Major Abdullah and Captain Amir on

floor 11 at the MOI where I was then permanently working. They told me that General Raad had been given a letter signed by Minister Baqir Jabr, stating that he had been retired from the police 'for the interests of the Iraqi people'. I was told by other Iraqi sources that the Minister was a member of SCIRI[11] and engaged in purging Sunni police officers from the Iraqi Police and replacing them with Shia Muslims. A number of Sunni senior officers had been murdered in targeted assassinations and a lot of people pointed the finger of suspicion at Minister Jabr. The pointed snub we all got when we left for Jordan six weeks earlier had materialised into destructive action. I felt sorry for the general who was a kind and firm man, but he had served his country and was better off retiring early than becoming another murder statistic in a list that was spiralling exponentially.

Mustafa Mohammad Salman al Jobouri appeared in court in Baghdad on 5 June 2006 with two other men. He denied any involvement with Margaret's kidnappers but admitted that a Sheikh who was an Imam at a mosque in south-east Baghdad gave him a plastic bag and told him to keep it in a safe place. He said the Sheikh would take it back from him after a little while but didn't say when. He kept the bag in his house but said that he didn't open it for a couple of months. He then told the court that he eventually opened the plastic bag to find the credentials of Margaret Hassan and her personal effects inside. He said that he returned to the Sheikh, who promised to take the bag back from him, but before he could return it the Sheikh disappeared and he believed he had left the country. He actually told me that he received the bag from another person who I subsequently found out was in fact closely associated with Sheikh Hussein. Mustafa denied any involvement in the murder but did say that he had spoken to Margaret during her captivity. He was found guilty of joining the group who kidnapped Margaret but not guilty of her murder. He was sentenced to life imprisonment. Two other men who had figured little in the enquiry were found not guilty of all charges.[12] This trial took place several weeks after my departure from Iraq and I was unaware of the trial date, had I known before I left, I would have asked to extend my mission to cover this case. Unfortunately, for a number of reasons, I was not kept in the loop about the trial by the IP as I could have been awkward about decisions being made around me and some thought it was better I was kept in the dark.

Long after my departure, Ali Lutfi Jassar al-Rawi aka Abu Rasha, an architect from Baghdad, was arrested by Iraqi and US forces in 2008. He had contacted the UK embassy in Baghdad after attempting to extort $1 million in return for disclosing the location of Margaret's body. He also claimed to be aware of detailed information about Margaret which was only known to her closest relatives – this was true. He used this knowledge to prove he knew the whereabouts of her body. He was handed over to the IP and admitted during interview that he knew where her body was and that he had attempted to obtain one million dollars to reveal the precise location of her remains. He made a full confession to the police but later retracted the confession at trial and claimed it had been extracted by torture. He told the court that he had received several beatings and was also given electric shocks during questioning. His defence lawyer maintained that he may have played a part in the blackmail plot but was not involved in her murder. Nonetheless, he was convicted of murder and sentenced to life imprisonment. He later appealed against his conviction and shortly before he was due to appear in court it was discovered that he had escaped from prison a month earlier during a riot in September 2009. Dr Baan Khaldoon Siddeeq al Rawi, the wife of Sheikh Hussein, is the sister of Ali Lutfi Jassar al-Rawi.

In January 2013, the *Irish Examiner* carried a story that in September 2012, Sheikh Hussein's wife had been stopped trying to leave Egypt, apparently for Kurdistan.[13] Whilst the Egyptian authorities were checking if she was in violation of the conditions under which she had residency in Egypt, it emerged that she was wanted for questioning about other crimes in Iraq. Unfortunately, she was not in detention at the time and evaded arrest. It was suspected that she was in company with her husband. Despite further searches for them, they could not be found. Their current whereabouts are unknown. In 2008, Mustafa Mohammad Salman al Jobouri appealed against his conviction and sentence and was released from prison that year. There are currently no persons in custody for the abduction and murder of Margaret Hassan.

I had a minor role in this case; primacy was held by the Iraqi Police, with the resources of the Metropolitan Police to assist wherever it was requested. Despite this, I wish to add some observations over the handling of this kidnap and murder with the sole purpose of reopening discussions on the correct way to deal with this type of crime.

The day after I had interviewed Mustafa al Jobouri, having been at the MOI for three consecutive days, the building was hit by a Katyusha rocket and twenty IP recruits killed nearby. Every month, the Iraqi security forces, including the police, were losing over 250 men and women in action and many more wounded. At the same time, over 500 Iraqi civilians were being killed every month and it was not uncommon for fifty or more civilians to be abducted and killed every day.[14] The insurgency was increasing in intensity, which it did until the US poured thousands more troops into the war in a phase known as 'the surge'. The kidnapping of Margaret Hassan took place when the fledgling democracy of Iraq was emerging from a long period of being under the heel of a dictator. The Coalition Provisional Authority (CPA), headed by Paul Bremer, took responsibility for running Iraq from 21 April 2003, shortly after the invasion, until it was dissolved on 28 June 2004, when power was handed to the Iraqi Interim government. The CPA was responsible for the executive, legislative and judicial authority for the whole country between these dates. Margaret was kidnapped on 19 October 2004 just three and a half months after this fledgling government took over and found itself dealing with what amounted to a full scale insurgency fired by religious hatred, a lot of score settling and tribal power battles. Democratic elections were not held until 30 January 2005.

Margaret Hassan held two passports, British and Iraqi. She was a dedicated professional humanitarian aid worker who had spent her life serving others. The strategic approach to her kidnapping by the UK government was to distance itself from her British nationality and emphasise her Iraqi citizenship and local connections. Much was made of the fact that she was born in the Republic of Ireland, but she had never considered herself Irish. This was backed up by a campaign described by an FCO spokesperson as 'personalisation and localisation' which was effected by a poster campaign and public demonstrations throughout Baghdad following her abduction. Furthermore, the primacy of the investigation was handed to the Iraqi Police, an organisation with much on its hands. The UK government had also taken the stance built up over years that it would 'not negotiate with terrorists'. This whole strategy was fundamentally flawed and doomed to failure.

Point one – Primacy. Margaret Hassan was a white Christian woman who spoke with an educated English accent. No matter what she did or how long she spent in Iraq the people who kidnapped her would only see the infidel woman. The fact that she was an outspoken opponent of the war would have meant nothing. There were five videos of Margaret sent to al Jazeera. The first was a non-sound picture of her with her identity documents displayed; the last video is of her murder. The second and third videos are appeals by Margaret for the British troops to be sent home and not to Baghdad. The third video adds demands for women prisoners in Iraq to be freed and the Care office to close. The fourth video shows Margaret faint after a short plea, then a man reading from the Koran. He is seen and heard to make demands for British troops to be withdrawn from Iraq and all women prisoners be released. The fifth video is of her murder. At no time on video or by any other means to my knowledge are demands made for money.

The kidnapping of Margaret appeared to be a politically motivated terrorist tactic taken by insurgent forces against the occupation of Iraq by the UK and against British interests and its citizens. This very self-evident fact was obscured in the early stages because the FCO appeared to consider that the motive could have been purely criminal and carried out for profit. It was in fact an act of war committed against the UK which encompassed kidnapping, torture and murder. It is therefore not only a crime, but a war crime and the action was not just against an individual; it was an act of terrorism against the UK. Both the FCO and the Metropolitan Police had concluded early in the enquiry, 'The security situation in Iraq and the lack of Iraqi police capacity have severely constrained any investigation of Margaret's kidnap and presumed murder. The Iraqi Police do not have the capability or experience to conduct a proper investigation.'[15] Primacy for the investigation of this offence should have been taken by the UK within the rules of engagement of Coalition forces with the Iraqi Police in support, not the other way round.

Point Two – Jurisdiction. Where a crime is committed outside the UK, it is generally beyond the jurisdiction of our courts to deal with it. However, if the *actus reus* (deliberate physical act) takes place in another country yet the criminal impact of that action is felt by person or persons in England and Wales, then it has been deemed to be within the jurisdiction of the Central Criminal Court.[16] The attack on the two towers on September 11 2001 was very much like the attack on Pearl Harbor in 1941. It brought the US into the Second World War, whereas 9/11 started a worldwide war, but one that is asymmetric in character. Kidnap is being used as a weapon of war to terrorise whole peoples and force elected governments to make decisions under duress. Margaret was kidnapped and murdered in Iraq, but the demands were made against the UK government in London. I do not know if this issue was ever considered in the early stages of her kidnap; if not it should have been. I would argue, therefore, that the principals of primacy and jurisdiction should have been tested. If it is found that our laws are failing to protect British subjects in this new age of protracted asymmetric warfare, then new laws need to be created to protect us all from the new and emerging dangers of the twenty-first century.

Point Three – Negotiating with terrorists and hostage takers. The UK government refused to engage in negotiations with the group. Tahseen received three phone calls, two of which came from Margaret's mobile phone number requesting contact with someone from the UK government to negotiate with. Tahseen, acting on instructions, told the caller that the UK government was not interested; this was all part of the policy of distancing the UK from Margaret. The contacts made evidenced desperation in the caller to negotiate with someone and a golden opportunity was missed because a flawed policy of not negotiating with terrorists was in effect. As a practical cop, it is in my DNA to negotiate. I talked a mentally disturbed man down off a roof in my early days and as a detective, I frequently negotiated with criminals over what they would admit and what they would not. The beat bobby every Friday and Saturday night negotiates with people to remain peaceful, not to disturb the peace and prevent fights before they start or get worse. This basic human interaction took centre stage on Good Friday 10 April 1998, when PM Tony Blair built on the good work of his predecessor John Major and brought peace to Ireland after thirty years of bloodshed. Deals were done, terrorists were released from prison early and some suspected terrorist killers received letters to confirm that they would not be prosecuted. To achieve this, the UK government had to speak to IRA terrorist commanders, no matter who government officials said they were. The result has been peace.

In the same way, the UK government should have engaged in negotiations with Margaret's kidnappers and it wasn't a hopeless case for a negotiator. The CARE office in Baghdad closed shortly after her kidnap and the Black Watch were only sent to Baghdad to cover the Fallujah operation for a limited period of time. Their return to Basra could have been an area for much talk with the kidnappers. The issue of the release of women prisoners could have also featured in negotiations and I am sure that some women were in any event due for release due to end of sentence or parole, or even amnesty. The jails in Iraq were bursting, there was room for movement. Much capital could have been made of such releases. Some areas could have been conceded without actually conceding anything in real terms. Margaret's kidnappers would have failed to comprehend why no one would negotiate with them and it is clear they were desperate to talk. Most of them were from the back alleys of Baghdad and the intricacies of British government foreign policy would be beyond them. Negotiation as a tool should never be taken off the table; the gains would at least have resulted in gathering intelligence information (which could have been enormous) and if the negotiations had failed, then at least they would have failed whilst daring greatly. Negotiating is about engaging with hostage takers, not submitting to them, failing to negotiate is a recipe for failure.

Point four – Ransom. When a ransom is paid it suggests to the kidnappers that their actions are a lucrative source of income and the sums involved are enormous. For people who have little, the prospect of getting their hands on millions of dollars will make the risk worth it. Successful kidnapping operations will breed more confidence and further kidnaps will invariably take place. Kidnapping is a veritable industry in Iraq, due to the lucrative returns and failure of the police to deal with it. Furthermore, the payment of a ransom is to provide an enemy with additional funds to buy more weapons and more people will suffer.

Unfortunately, for this policy to succeed every nation has to sign up to not paying a ransom. European governments do appear to pay ransoms despite official denials and I have little doubt that commercial companies also pay ransoms in various parts of the world where criminals and militias carry out kidnappings for profit. Despite this, I do think that the position of the UK government not to pay ransoms is correct. The interest of the state in this aspect should therefore take precedence over the interests of the individual and family, hard though that might be. This issue should be separated out from the tactic of negotiation which is a separate matter and should not be intertwined with the payment of ransoms.

Point Five – Justice. I do not know if the Iraqi Police Service are pursuing the arrest of Sheikh Hussein, his wife and members of the gang. The UK government have made few promises to catch these killers, appearing to have left it all to the Iraqis who are engaged in a fight for survival at the time of writing (2016). The UK government has demonstrated its determination to bring savage killers to justice, as has been seen with the targeted killing of murderers from the so called Islamic State. Why has the UK government not pursued Margaret's killers with the same determination? The likelihood of detection has always been a major factor in the prevention of crime. When British citizens are killed anywhere in the world it should be the duty of the British government to bring the killers to justice, wherever they may be hiding.

Point six – Review. The police routinely review murder enquiries and if a crime of murder is undetected, the whole investigation is subject to a review, usually from an outside force to give independence and objectivity to such a procedure. The process is designed not around blaming somebody for failing to charge an offender, but a double check on trying to find the killer from clues which the initial team may have missed and learning 'best practice'. I am unaware if the FCO have carried out an independent review of the kidnap and murder of Margaret; if so it has not been made public. I am afraid to say that my assessment of this and other kidnappings is that the UK embassy in Iraq's main priority at this particular time was to protect the policy of the UK government; the victim was very much secondary. I also sensed from the police involved at the time of her kidnap a decided lack of flair and what amounted to an exercise in finding as many reasons as they could as to why they should not deal with the case, instead of grabbing it by the throat and getting on with the job.

I sincerely hope that one day Margaret's body will be recovered, her family be given back her remains and she be given a dignified Christian burial. Undoubtedly her soul is with God.

Chapter Seventeen
Brian Tilley

In June 2005, I was working in an office at the UK embassy which had been made available for the UK police by a member of the embassy who clearly thought the police were well below their social and intellectual level. Colin was also going to commence working permanently in Baghdad, as he wanted to centralise more of the UK police effort in the capital and I had endeavoured to increase our office space. Whilst I was trying to sort out a number of logistical problems like transport, communications and the correct body armour for our police personnel, not the flimsy stuff we had been issued with, Constable Peters came into the office.

'Hello, sir,' he said. 'Do you know a Detective Superintendent James from Dorset?'

I replied, 'Phil James, of course I do.'

Phil James had been a sergeant in Boscombe many years before and had led a squad of six constables who worked in plain clothes arresting street drug dealers, pickpockets and handbag thieves. As we were both sergeants at that time, we worked closely together on many of the same cases which continued throughout our careers. He was a very practical, handsome chap, tall and gaunt with a mass of black wavy hair. He made it onto CID and when I was the detective chief inspector (DCI) in Bournemouth he was the DCI in Poole; he loved to belittle my division by saying I didn't have much to do all day as Bournemouth was the 'blue rinse' capital of the South. Needless to say, his acid comments were batted back over the net with equal force. Constable Peters then went on to explain that he had received an e mail from Phil concerning the murder of Brian Tilley, a former special forces man who had lived in Dorset and had been murdered along with six Iraqis in Baghdad in May of the previous year. Brian Tilley had been working in the private security sector in Iraq and was a valued member of his company. He had formed friendships with a number of the local people, some of whom lived in the al Doura area of the city. Whilst on a visit to these friends, with whom he stayed overnight, five or six men burst into the house, stole jewellery and cash and ended up by killing the six occupants, including Brian.

'Why has this taken since May last year?' I asked.

Constable Peters announced with some concern, 'It appears that the IP are the murderers and they don't seem to want to prosecute their own.' I asked him to give me all the paperwork he had (which wasn't much) and I decided to get involved.

I contacted Phil who was glad to hear from me, as I think he had experienced difficulties in communications with those involved in the investigation or monitoring of it. After the usual police ritual of trading insults when old colleagues make contact, he explained that they had received the body of Brian Tilley back in Dorset on 24 May 2004. He was a Poole man so it was the responsibility of the Poole Coroner to enquire into his cause of death. I learned that Dr Allen Anscombe, an accomplished Home Office pathologist with whom I had worked numerous times in the past, had carried out the autopsy and he confirmed that Mr Tilley had died as a result of multiple gunshot wounds to his back and stomach. The toes on his right foot had also been badly injured. Phil explained to me that the case had stalled somewhere in the Iraqi judicial system despite a survivor of the shooting having made a statement. He asked me to do whatever I could to kick-start the investigation.

A young teenager aged sixteen or seventeen called Sarah had survived the attack and had made a full statement after a patrol of US army soldiers had rescued her a little while after the murders. This is what she said.

At about 8am on the morning of the 14 May 2004, Sarah was lying in bed in her room at her house in al Doura. Asleep in other rooms were her mother, Raha al Obaibi; her auntie, Rasha; her friend, Imaan; the owner of the house an Iraqi man called Nassir and his sister in law, Bushra. Also asleep in another room was a British man now known to be Brian Tilley. He had long untidy hair and was of swarthy complexion which enabled him to blend in well with the locals. Sarah said that she jumped awake after hearing very loud banging on the front door which was then forced open and five men dressed in Iraqi Police uniform burst in. They shouted for everyone to obey them and make no trouble and her mother was pushed into her bedroom followed by Nassir. Acting in a very aggressive manner, the five Iraqi policemen then proceeded to ransack the bedroom taking cash and jewellery as they found it. Whilst they were rummaging through a set of drawers in the room, Brian Tilley made an appearance having been woken up by the commotion. Being a law abiding Englishman, he must have thought that the police were carrying out a search for drugs with a warrant or searching for stolen goods. It would not have occurred to him that in fact it was the police in broad daylight who were carrying out a robbery in full uniform.

The police were surprised and said to him in Arabic, 'What are you doing here?'

He showed them his identification cards and three policemen took him into the kitchen whilst Sarah remained in the bedroom with her mother. Nassir crept close to the kitchen door when they were left alone and whispered that the British man was being tortured, he was beaten and then shot in the foot with a pistol. The IP then came out of the kitchen and threatened Nassir. They demanded that he give them the keys to his safe but he refused. Sarah hurled some insults at them and they shot above her head. Two of the IP were left to guard Brian, who was by now badly injured, whilst their accomplices moved all the women into the bedroom together. The IP shouted again at Nassir for the safe keys and the ignition keys to a BMW which was parked outside but he defiantly refused. It cost him his life and they shot him a number of times. Brian, who had been kept apart from the others was then heard to shout 'No' before being shot in the stomach and back several times; he died on the floor. Two of the attackers then entered the bedroom where the women had been kept and rattled off a hail of bullets, killing Sarah's mother, her auntie and the other two women. When Raha had realised what was about to happen, she threw herself in an act of desperation across her daughter's body and soaked up the bullets intended for her. Sarah fell unconscious, bleeding from the neck and was left for dead by the cold blooded and ruthless killers. The policemen then left the house and drove off in the BMW, which had been parked outside and which had in fact belonged to Brian; their pockets were full of stolen cash and jewellery. They also took a number of weapons that Brian had brought with him, including two chrome plated pistols, a Glock pistol, an MP5 and an AK Skorpion carbine. He had also been in possession of thousands of dollars in cash when he was killed as he was due to go on leave that day. He should have flown out of the country the day before but his flight had been cancelled; his luck had finally run out.

Brian Tilley was a former Royal Marine and had spent twenty of his twenty-two years service in the 'Special Boat Service'. This is one of Britain's most famous special forces regiments. He received the Queen's Gallantry medal in 1996 and took part in covert operations in Northern Ireland and the first Gulf War. He was also involved in training special forces in the Middle East and was engaged in anti-drug smuggling operations in South America. He was an expert mountain climber, having conquered K2 and after he left the armed forces he worked as a bodyguard, for, among other people, the celebrity footballer David Beckham and his wife. He went to work in Iraq after the second Gulf War as did many former soldiers; war after all was his profession. He was an accomplished man of action, who had achieved in his forty-seven years what most men can only dream about.

Shortly after 8am on the morning of 14 May 2004, Captain Brennan and Sergeant Duennes, with their patrol of US army 5th

Cavalry, arrived at the scene of carnage in al Doura having been called by the local IP. The soldiers quickly assessed the surroundings and carried out preliminary crime scene work, including photographing the bodies where they lay. All the victims were in nightwear other than Mr Tilley. They searched his body and found his British passport and were therefore able to quickly identify him. The IP told Captain Brennan and her patrol that a teenage girl had survived the shooting and was being treated in the nearby al Karkh hospital. The patrol went immediately to the hospital to speak to the survivor who was being treated for a bullet wound to the neck, but incredibly the bullet had not severed or impacted on any major arteries or organs. She immediately told the Americans that the people responsible for her shooting and the murder of her family and friends were rogue Iraqi policemen and worse still, she had seen two or three of them in the hospital as she was brought in. She was terrified that they were looking for her and wanted to silence her permanently. Captain Brennan took swift and decisive action and removed her immediately to another medical facility where she could be kept safe from the killers.

The 5th Cavalry owned the 'battle space' of the al Doura area of Baghdad. This was a highly dangerous slum area crisscrossed by alleys and lanes. It was a hive of insurgent and criminal activity. In order to know their area, the 5th Cavalry had very smartly organised a system of photographing all the local police and issuing every one with US-issue bespoke identity cards. The army were aware that insurgents regularly wore counterfeit IP uniforms to carry out killings of their rivals and coalition forces and making sure they knew who was who on their patch was one way of countering this threat. Captain Brennan built up a rapport with Sarah and asked her if she would be able to recognise the killers from a series of photographs she had on a laptop, Sarah agreed to try. She was shown 200 photographs of the local IP taken by the 5th Cavalry and identified five policemen, who, it transpired, all worked together at the local police station in al Doura. Captain Brennan having done her job with panache then had to hand the case over to the police to investigate, but to ensure the investigation was carried out with propriety she made sure it went into the hands of some US police mentors who were deployed alongside her regiment. It was these police officers who obtained the first written account from Sarah of the massacre she had witnessed. Phil James later met Captain Brennan, who he regarded as a very professional military officer and he said of Sergeant Duennes, 'He was your typical career soldier who spent his time ensuring the success of his responsible officer.'

After Sarah had made a full recovery, she was discharged from hospital into the safe-keeping of Captain Brennan and the 5th Cavalry. However, she was rightly concerned for Sarah's safety. She found a solution to this problem when Andy Edwards, Brian's immediate supervisor in the same security company, agreed to look after Sarah until court proceedings had been completed. Brian was a popular man and the small band of former special forces soldiers would do all they could in helping bring the killers to justice. Phil James then became involved in the investigation after Brian's body had been received back in Dorset a few days after the murders. He made contact with Andy Edwards and Phil made arrangements to interview Sarah himself and take a statement from her which would be acceptable in a British court. The meeting was to take place in Amman, not at the embassy, as one of the FCO types was concerned that she might ask for political asylum whilst on UK territory; frankly, I wish she had. Phil flew out to Jordan in November 2004. Unfortunately, when he showed up to meet Mr Edwards it was discovered that Sarah had gone missing. She had given her minders the slip and disappeared into the night. The lure of a peaceful and safer Jordan had been too much for her to resist. Phil returned to Dorset empty-handed and the major piece of evidence in the case was missing in Amman.

Now that I was fully aware of the facts, my first job was to get this investigation moving again. I needed to track down the US police advisor who had been working in the Major Crime Unit (MCU) and who had written down the first statement made by Sarah. As well as deploying 150,000 military personnel to Iraq in 2004, the United States also deployed 800 former or serving police officers. These were scattered throughout the country, but the main bulk were stationed in and around Baghdad. They interacted with the IP as trainers at the police academy; mentoring at various IP facilities throughout the country and formed Police Transition Teams where they were embedded with the military. They enjoyed far greater freedom of movement than I did and they visited the IP in their stations or in the field on a daily basis. One of their tasks was to mentor and advise the IP MCU based in the MOI under the command of Major General Tariq al Bedawi, the deputy Minister of Interior (there were seven Deputy Ministers of Interior).

The man I was after was Vince Madrid, a tall, competent, self-assured former detective who I met in the Adnan Palace, where I also had a desk, on 16 June 2005. Vince still worked permanently with the Major Crimes Unit advising on investigations. He told me that following the identifications made from photographs by Sarah, she had attended several identification parades at the MOI and picked out three policemen who she said were responsible. Vince had personally witnessed these identification procedures and said they were conducted in a fair and legal manner. The three men were all charged with murder and taken to appear before Judge Zuhair. Sarah attended the court and told the judge everything that had happened, all in accordance with the earlier written statement she had made. After enquiring into the case for less than a day and to the surprise of the US policemen, he acquitted all the accused policemen of murder. In his judgement he said that the witness Sarah lived in the same neighbourhood as the accused and that she only picked them out because she recognised them as local police. He also said that he had information that she had argued with them in the past and she had an ongoing dispute with the local police. As a result of these factors, he didn't believe her account of the events.

Vince and I both agreed that this was utterly disgusting and it was obvious that the killers were being protected. I asked about ballistic evidence and enquired regarding seizure of spent bullets, cartridges and so on; it appeared that the IP who attended the scene carried out only a minimal crime scene examination and they may have retained some cartridge cases. The only two bullets seized were two spent bullets seized by soldiers of the 5th Cavalry and nobody was really sure where they were found. I did not know if any bullets had been recovered from Mr Tilley and didn't want to assume that any had been, as it had been drummed into my head years ago in detective training to never assume anything.

'How about seizure of the suspect's weapons and test firing against the bullets that have been found?' I suggested.

Vince agreed that it was an obvious forensic procedure and would get it done if he could secure the guns, bullets and cartridges. I contacted Phil, who pledged that if we could get the firearms to Dorset he would arrange the forensic examination. If we could find the bullet or cartridge case, we could forensically link it to the weapon and then trace the weapon to the policeman who signed it out that day or had it on permanent issue. If that was one of the policemen picked out by Sarah, then we would have corroborated her identification and the whole case would stack up convincingly. This was all very basic detective work, but this was Iraq and was anything but simple.

The police in Iraq had for many years been the poor relation in the matter of internal security. There had been no forensic science service and the main effort in investigating crime was to drag a suspect into a police station and obtain a confession. In fairness, the police I joined in 1971 had a heavy over-reliance on confession evidence. It was not until after far too many miscarriages of justice in the 1970s and 1980s, which had caused juries to distrust police confession evidence, that the service geared up its forensic crime scene work and other evidence collection methods so that it no longer had to rely on confessions alone.

I went away for leave in late July 2005 and when I returned in early August the insurgency was getting even worse. I met Jo at the embassy and she briefed me about events which had occurred in my absence. The worst from our point of view was that of Inspector Aldous, a police trainer in Basra who was on his way to a meeting when two EFPs were detonated as his convoy passed. An EFP is an explosively formed projectile comprising a copper slug fired from a metal tube which heats up on ignition into a molten mass. It can burn through heavy armour. The country of origin for these deadly roadside weapons was Iran. One CRG (ex RUC) bodyguard was killed instantly and another bodyguard (former Royal Marine) died shortly after. To make matters worse, the IP attended the scene of the explosion and fired their guns into the dead guard and stole his glock pistol, boots and wedding ring. I asked myself what on earth was I doing here?

I met up with Vince Madrid and his partner Mike McCarthy, another former US police officer, a few days later and they told me that they had spoken to General Raad who was responsible for the day to day running of the MCU and he had agreed (under pressure from Vince and Mike) to have a look at the case, but said he couldn't do anything unless the Deputy Minister of Interior gave permission to reopen the investigation. If the case was to be reopened, he said he would want a new statement from Sarah and for her again to be produced in court to a new investigating judge. Therein was a further problem, in that she was a crucial witness and there was no forensic or other evidence, at least as yet; the whole thing hinged on her. The fact that she had made it to Jordan meant to me that it was very unlikely that she would return to Iraq; why should she? Her life was in danger and her family were all dead. They also told me that during the course of their enquiries, they had heard from Mr Edwards, Brian's boss, that one of the murdered women may have been having a sexual relationship with a senior Iraqi politician and a member of the Iraqi National Congress. This rumour was traced to a friend of the brother of Imam, one of those murdered, but it seemed to me to be rather vague. Sarah was interviewed about this rumour and she said she knew the Iraqi politician because he was frequently on the television. However, she was absolutely adamant that he had never visited the house nor was any mention ever made of his name. This suggestion was never substantiated and was tenuous at best.

This case seemed to be going nowhere and the IP were finding every reason not to investigate it. Having carried out several cold case reviews, I knew that over time relationships change. It seemed there had been no interviews carried out on the policemen at al Doura police station; most would have known the suspects and they may have even talked about what they had done to some of their friends and colleagues. After all, it is not every day that between three and five policemen in a local neighbourhood police station go out and kill six people and rob the place of gold, thousands of dollars in cash and some highly desirable firearms. With all the information I had, I needed to go to the top man in charge of crime investigation, the Deputy Minister of Interior, Major General Tariq al Bedawi, which I did on the 8 August 2005. The Minister told me that he didn't know much about the case other than that the surviving witness was fourteen and was therefore in his view too young to be believed. He said that she was a bad girl and in any event the word of one female is not good enough because two female witnesses were needed. I was aware that Islamic law required two female witnesses to give evidence before it would have credibility, whereas witness evidence from one male was enough. I did question with him the validity of this unfair rule in the modern age, to which he quipped back that it was his culture and they do things differently; he viewed western culture with laws allowing homosexuals to marry and adopt children as equally at odds with Iraqi ways. I was not going to get into a fight with the Minister and returned the conversation to other crime investigations ongoing.

I tried several more times to try to get the Minister to reopen the case but failed each time. He was in an entrenched position and I was getting nowhere. By chance, in late August of that year, I met with Brigadier Ahmed, who was the chief of Internal Control or what we would know back in Britain as the police complaints department. He was a tall imposing man with jet black hair and the obligatory moustache. He was extremely well dressed in a smart tailored suit, silk shirt and tie. He was wearing a large pair of sunglasses in his rather dark office which I never saw him without. Behind his desk was a door partially open beyond which I saw a bed. I found that a lot of IP senior officers had beds in their offices or adjoining rooms. Many of them slept at the MOI during the week, as insurgents were carrying out assassinations of senior IP officers on a regular basis as they travelled to and from work. He was very concerned for his security having survived seven attempts on his life and on one of these his driver had been killed. He was also concerned that one of the Deputy Ministers of Interior was trying to reduce the size of his department by moving out twenty investigators. He showed me an order dated 11 July ordering the transfer which gave no reason for the moves. He showed me another letter from the same person offering him the job of head of criminal intelligence for which he would be paid more, which he remarked was a sweetener but he wanted to stay where he was because he believed in what he was doing to improve the IPS by trying to remove corrupt policemen. I took his concerns to my American friends, Col. Lance Lane and others, on floor seven of the MOI. They all understood that there was a move to stifle investigations into corrupt members of the IPS and they were also concerned about the threats against Brigadier Ahmed. Fortunately, they had the resources and the clout to ensure his security was enhanced both at home and during his travelling to and from work.

Over the months I met with Brigadier Ahmed quite frequently and I felt I might receive more help from him than anyone else with the unsolved murder of Brian Tilley. When I judged the moment right, I brought up the case and asked him to look into it. I discussed with him various lines of enquiry which could be taken, including interviewing the officers who worked at al Doura, but not the suspects, to see if anyone would confidentially spill the beans on them. Brigadier Ahmed, true to his word, dug into the case. He carried out some research on the suspects, one of whom, Lieutenant Hammad Kareem al Joboury, was regarded as lazy and frequently absent from work; Captain Omar al Samara was suspected of attacks on coalition forces; and Captain Hammad Ismail, the last of those to stand accused, was killed in al Doura on 8 September 2005 by insurgents.

At a further meeting in April 2006, Brigadier Ahmed showed me his findings from the initial investigation. No attempt had been made to find witnesses, not even to speak to the local residents in the same street. Little or no forensic work was done, the cartridge cases had been lost and the weapons used by the police in al Doura had been replaced by new ones. There was no forensic or indeed any other evidence. Despite his best efforts, Sarah could not be found. Judge Zuhair was suspected of corruption and had released the suspected killers without permission from the senior judge. The case was a mess and was not going anywhere. The insurgent attacks in Iraq were continuing their upward spiral and on the last day I saw Brigadier Ahmed, I witnessed an attack on a coalition convoy coming to the MOI and could clearly see vehicles slewed across an approach road and on fire. One American had been killed and another seriously wounded by an EFP, the use of which was now becoming common. My office on the eleventh floor of the MOI gave a grand view of the mayhem all around.

Despite Brigadier Ahmed's best intentions, the case never moved forward. There was no forensic evidence, the witness Sarah was never traced, there was no willingness from the Deputy Minister of Interior to bring the perpetrators to justice; after all, the sole surviving witness was in his words a 'bad girl'. Phil James attended the inquest held by the Coroner in Poole on 7 November 2007. He told the Coroner about the many efforts made to bring Brian's killers to justice, but how those efforts had eventually failed. He went on record to say that Sarah's identification of the suspects was 'accurate and adequate enough for a court in the UK'. Dorset Deputy Coroner Jonathon Morrissey recorded a verdict of unlawful killing.

Chapter Eighteen
Don't Mention The (Civil) War

In early June 2005, I was invited to a reception for the new incoming ambassador, Sir William Patey, at his residence in the Green Zone. It lies in an area of the city where senior Ba'ath party members had lived and was replete with small watercourses and well-tended lawns, a status symbol in a city where the average day time temperature in the summer is 45 degrees and there is no rain between April to October. The residence is really an extension of the ambassador's office, where he received politicians from the Prime Minister downward and numerous foreign dignitaries. Very noticeable was a huge chandelier in the entrance hall which opened out into large rooms on both sides with marble floors. I got on well with most of the embassy staff, other than a woman in the administration department who I was having trouble with concerning office space, telephones, transport and just about everything else. I found the people from the Department for International Development (DFID) a bit stand-offish. They were more the sort of *Guardian* reader types who automatically see the police as some kind of repressive arm of the state and they tended to remain aloof, sometimes it was all I could do to get a 'good morning' out of them as we passed in the corridor. DFID was the creation of the Labour government and the result of severing the aid work carried out by the UK government from its political objectives as pursued by the FCO. DFID wished to remain above the mucky political level and do its work in a non-partisan way and not attach political strings to aid giving. USAID, the American equivalent, gives billions of dollars in aid but there is always a benefit to the American people, particularly the economy. Why supply Toyota vehicles to a third world country benefiting workers in Japan instead of supplying Land Rovers to benefit British workers?

Whilst at this cheese and wine party, I met two FCO mid-level political officers and mentioned that I would be going on leave in a month or two's time. I told them that I had always had a good relationship with my local press and suggested I let the local *Dorset Echo* know all about the good work going on out here and what we, the British, were doing amid the civil war raging all around us. I almost created apoplexy with my two new-found and short-lived friends. There is no civil war going on, I was told; this is merely people settling old scores after the fall of a dictator. A civil war, I was told, is where armies face each other and the country splits into separate entities and groups. That was not the case here and things would settle down after the initial upheaval. I didn't argue with that, I had obviously got it wrong and who was a country copper to disagree with people half my age but doubtless twice as bright as I was?

Six weeks later, I saw Gerry Burke in the Adnan Palace; he was concerned about some open source non classified emails he had received over the last few days. Bodies were turning up in the Baghdad sewage plant, or city tip, with their hands bound behind their backs and shot in the head. On several occasions, between twenty to fifty men were taken from specific neighbourhoods or places of work; they were all men and all Sunnis. There was no effort made to hide the bodies and the fact that they were left at the city rubbish dump or sewage plant sent out a contemptuous and terrifying message to the families, tribes and group from which the victims had come.

On 25 August 2015, thirty-six men were taken from their homes in Baghdad and found a couple of days later in Kut. They were all bound with metal or plastic handcuffs and shot in the head. All the bodies were in a line and some showed signs of torture, with acid having possibly been used. I was informed by a source of mine that the unit involved in the abduction and murder of these men was the al Bakhan (Volcano) Brigade. They were seen to be wearing Iraqi Police (IP) uniforms and driving IP Dodge trucks painted blue and white and with the word 'police' painted on them. If it walks like a duck and it quacks like a duck, then more than likely it is a duck. And these were not any old police these were the 'Special Police Commandos,' a 5,000 strong force of gun-wielding, intimidating men whose number had been swelled by mass inductions of untrained Militia men, principally the Badr Brigade, the military wing of the Iran based Shia Islamic party, SCIRI.

Gerry and I agreed that for the minimum of effort, drones could hover over these sites with a rapid reaction force on standby to intercept the murderers and/or troops could be dug in around the locations. The bodies were being found at such a frequent rate that a result would have been achieved within a short period of time. Gerry saw a US army colonel who was an aide de camp to a war fighting US general and made that proposal to him.

The colonel took the suggestion away with him but a day or two later, having apparently discussed the idea with his general, he replied, 'It's an Iraqi problem. Iraq was a sovereign nation and we could not interfere.'

Gerry added to me, 'It sounded like a company line.' He tried again a little while later with a different colonel but back came the same reply.

It was around this time that I attended a meeting at the Adnan Palace chaired by Lt. General David Petraeus, who was leading the Multi-National Security Transition Command – Iraq (MNSTC-I). The task of this huge organisation was to train and equip the new Iraqi army and to reform and rebuild the police. This also included infrastructure projects involving the building of police stations, army facilities and border forts; the amount of US dollars involved was into billions. The general had recently built a team to work at the MOI on a daily basis which was engaged in helping the Ministry restructure. Once again, I was in the right place at the right time and by the end of that day I was asked to work as a police advisor on this team, which had a

British brigadier in charge. The unit, which comprised about forty personnel, was principally staffed by US military and civilian experts. Within the team, there were specialists from everything including human resources, recruiting, pay, training, policy, statistics and every other department a police headquarters cum Home Office would require. The particularly good news for me was that I was to move out to Forward Operating Base (FOB) Shield and live there permanently. The national police academy training establishment was within the FOB and the MOI was just outside so I had less daily travel. However, it was necessary to return to the Green Zone most weekends, as I had contingent business and meetings with Colin and others to attend. A few days later and with some other police advisors working at the police academy, I moved house to the FOB, where I also met Inspector Bob Lamburne, that most highly professional Crime Scene Manager with whom I had worked in Kosovo. He was setting up a whole forensic examination department and training centre at the academy which would serve the Iraqi Police nationally and was funded by the UK government.

We all lived in a concrete block of single storey rooms with a communal bathroom, there being about fifteen of us altogether including the CRG guards. I was always amused to hear them playing shoot-em-up computer games when they were relaxing. I shared my room with a six foot four inch barrel-chested Texan called 'Duke' Bodich. He was a great guy, a senior law enforcement officer from Houston, a Vietnam War veteran and a member of the US Marine reserve. We regularly went to work in the MOI together; he carried a combat shotgun, a berretta semi-automatic pistol and an M4 carbine – he was all Texan. I had an office on the eleventh floor and at least once or twice a week had long meetings with the Deputy Minister of Interior, Ali Ghalib. This association lasted for the remainder of my mission to May 2006. I managed to resolve a number of policy and procedure issues with the Deputy Minister, which included banning the police from taking part in politics (in name at least), frequency of pay, war widows' pay and streamlining lines of command and defining areas of responsibility. Crimes tended to be dealt with by whichever unit arrived first at a crime scene and this could be any one of seven different departments, all operating within their own stove pipe and not sharing a great deal of information. There was a lot of work to do. At the conclusion of our meetings, I would agree a time and date for our next get together and he would always add, 'Insha'Allah, Insha'Allah.' This means 'if God wills it' and is fundamental to the faith of Muslims, as it demonstrates a submission to God's will; things will only happen if God wills it so.

I also worked with a lot of other different Iraqi officers. One in particular I saw frequently was Colonel Ahmad, who was helping spread my simple card index collators project. I met with him most mornings at the MOI and we enjoyed a cup of tea whilst talking about the latest news – mainly bad. Iraqis don't have milk in their tea. 'Milk is for babies,' he told me, laughing. Colonel Ahmad was a tall, slim, dark-skinned man with soulful eyes and always immaculately dressed. The more I saw of him the more he took me into his confidence. He told me that an uncle of his was on the pack of playing cards issued by the Americans to identify and arrest senior former regime Ba'ath party members, so I guess he himself would not have made it to colonel unless he had been acceptable to the party. In early September, over an early morning cup of tea, or chai as the Iraqis say, he looked more worried than normal and told me that three men, all Badr brigade, had been arrested in possession of rifles with silencers and were thought to be an assassination team. He said that by orders of the Minister of Interior they had all been released. He also told me that members of his department were being recruited by Iranian agents.

Bayan Jabr (also known as Baqir Jabr al-Zubeidi) was the Minister of Interior, having been appointed in April 2005, the role being similar to that of the British Home Secretary. However, unlike the Home Secretary who does not get involved in operational police decision-making, the Minister of Interior was very involved in operational policing matters. He had broken free of his US mentor, Steve Casteel, a US senior law enforcement official and had been the senior advisor to the MOI from October

2003 to July 2005. Steve was a larger than life character with a wealth of experience in the FBI behind him. He knew his job and did his best to help his interlocutor. However, after Steve left in July 2005, a former American ambassador took his place but he lacked Steve's charisma and force. Bayan Jabir flexed his muscles and the new advisor was pushed out into a side office and was eventually side-lined totally. Colonel Ahmad was becoming increasingly worried about the Minister, who he believed was engaged on a policy of removing all Sunnis and definitely anyone with a hint of a connection to the former regime. This was also something I had heard from other sources.

A month later, I called into Colonel Ahmad's office to discuss some routine business and found him to be frightened and distressed. 'What's the matter?' I asked, but he looked over my shoulder at an assistant hovering in his room.

I turned and spoke to him. 'Would you leave us, please? I have important business to discuss with the colonel. One of your very senior men has told me it is a secret and for the colonel only.' The assistant left the room. 'What is it?' I said

'I'm on the Minister's death list,' he said. 'I'm sure it's right, it's my business to know all these things. What shall I do?' he asked.

I had no hesitation. For years, I have stressed the importance to witnesses or victims of rape and abuse to attend court and give evidence, to stand up and be counted, but against all my former beliefs I said, 'Get out as quick as you can, where are your family?'

He said, 'At home.'

I said, 'Get them out today and you follow as soon as they cross the [Jordanian] border, don't come in tomorrow, wait at a friend's house until you are clear to go.'

He nodded solemnly. All this was conducted in hushed whispers and as I left, I smiled at his aide, who I didn't trust one bit. The very next day I strolled down the corridor to say good morning to the colonel as was my way, when his aide approached me and said that the colonel hadn't arrived yet. I put on a look of surprise, but was elated and worried at the same time. I called back at his office a couple of times during the day to be met by his increasingly worried staff. The day following, I called again to be told by his aide, in a very surprised manner, that the colonel was in Jordan with his family and would not be coming back. I acted dumb, an act that seems to come easily to me! Inside, I was elated. Colonel Ahmad was a good loyal servant of all the people of Iraq and at least he may live to see his country in better days.

The abductions and murders continued throughout the country that summer and involved diverse groups with different agendas.[17] Added to the chaos were an abundance of criminals who took full advantage of the instability and turned kidnapping and ransoming of hostages into a growing industry. At the end of August, almost a thousand Shia pilgrims died following a stampede on a bridge in Baghdad. They had panicked when someone had cried out that there was a suicide bomber in their midst and the resulting crush had devastating consequences. Shia pilgrims and mosques had been the target of Sunni extremists for some time. Reprisals followed this catastrophe with blood upon blood. I was actually in Hassan AK's office on the day of these deaths and he said, 'The civil war will only deepen now.'

There were increasing tensions within the MOI towards coalition forces and the looks became blacker. I noticed that on some levels in the building, women police personnel had been employed to search female visitors. These women were now veiled and wore thin gloves over their hands, to hide their flesh and finger nails despite the oppressive heat, a Shia trait. Even my Deputy Minister, Ali Ghalib, went on the Hajj to Mecca, as did many other senior leaders; the Shia hold was increasing its grip on the MOI. I remember at this time I was with my friend, a US police advisor, John Bozicevich, and as we left the MOI a sand storm blew in. Now a sand storm suggests sand, but in Iraq the sand is more like talcum powder and it gets into everything. Worse still, the visibility gets down to a few feet and on this occasion the whole sky and area around became blood red. With the sound of explosions from car bombs and mortars in the distance breaking the eerie silence, it felt like this world and the next were colliding into each other.

Chief Superintendent Marks was a former RUC officer and an

expert in counter insurgency policing. He had been specially selected by the FCO with strong representations from Colin to help the Iraqi police collect and action crime intelligence at the state level. Amongst other things, he got to know Col. Stewart, Col. Lane and Lt. Col. Moss who all worked on floor seven at the MOI and who, by coincidence, I also knew well. Col. Stewart was a rugged and handsome rugby player, Col. Lance Lane was shorter, about 5ft 7in tall, but a tough wiry man of the 101st Airborne. He also wore a dagger at his side plus his usual sidearm. Lt Col Moss was a quieter more taciturn type and a cavalry officer. It was they who told me of the deteriorating situation inside the MOI; they had experienced being 'shouldered' or being deliberately bumped into by Iraqi policemen whilst they walked about the corridors. They were running an intelligence cell with the IP and Ch. Supt. Marks linked into this from his end of the project. I guess because I knew them all, Marks asked me to accompany him on an inspection of a facility in the Karrada area of Baghdad known as 'The Bunker'. Marks told me that there was suspicion that the IP were detaining suspects there and torturing them, our job was to carry out preliminary enquiries with the units there and try to establish what they were actually doing. When a detective carries out the first interview of a suspect, the strategy is usually to ask open questions which leave the suspect free to elaborate or describe their actions without the interviewer inhibiting their replies by challenging their answers too much. Thus, an account of the suspect's movements is gained which can be followed up by closer questioning in successive interviews. I was delighted at being asked to take part in this operation as it sounded like real investigative work.

On Monday 24 October 2005, together with Chief Supt. Marks, Lt. Col. Moss and elements of the US army, I attended the Bunker to carry out what was a prearranged inspection for which the Minister of Interior had given his permission. The building was about twenty years old and had been built as an air raid shelter and command post, hence its name. It had a ground floor and an upper floor and it was believed to have a number of subterranean floors. We were met with great courtesy by the senior Iraqi officer in charge of this facility, Engineer Ahmed and his team. Chief Supt. Marks went with Engineer Ahmed and Lt. Col Moss on an inspection of the building whilst I, with Major Johnson, spoke to Brigadier Hammed and Colonel Mehdi who were in charge of investigations. They told us that they received their orders direct from the Minister of Interior, which could involve cases of terrorism, corruption and other major crime. Brig. Hammed considered that Islamist extremists were responsible for the greatest amount of terrorism in the country followed by former regime elements (FRE), with profit-seeking criminals a long way behind that. He said that the majority of these came from Syria and Palestine. He firmly believed that Ba'athists in Syria were fermenting the situation. This played into the narrative of Syrian involvement on the one hand and Iranian interference on the other, leading to a proxy war being fought in Iraq, not that this was a civil war of course. A long conversation took place about the numbers of police personnel engaged on these investigations, cases dealt with and their day-to-day activities. They said that detainees were held for questioning at this facility for up to three days and then handed into the custody of an investigating judge. I asked about how they gathered evidence prior to an arrest and the use of surveillance. They told me that they did not have dedicated surveillance vehicles, but used the private cars belonging to their men. I got the impression that their modus operandi was to receive information from the MOI and doubtless other sources, then to arrest the suspect and search their house and rely on interrogation to produce the evidence. I asked to look in their exhibit store to see the kind of hard evidence they collected but was told the person with the key to the room had not reported for work that day!

I asked to look at the cell block where prisoners were held. There was a conference between Brig. Hammed and Col. Mehdi which resulted in another brigadier drifting into view who introduced himself as Ali Sadiq. He was a very tall, imposing man with very dark almost black skin, unlike the average Iraqi. He showed us two rooms which looked like offices. They had tables and chairs and were quite pristine. Most cells have a fixed bed, a mattress, a toilet and are secured by a thick steel door.

Brig. Ali Sadiq had experienced a tragic life; he told us that four of his brothers had been killed in a Shia uprising in the early 1990s and that his son had been injured in a road accident, resulting in brain damage. His mother was killed in the same incident. Unfortunately, the collision involved a US army convoy, but he spoke highly of the Americans and the medical treatment they gave to his son. He added that in the 1990s, he had taken part in a failed assassination attempt on the life of Uday Hussein. He was arrested, tied up and had both his legs broken by Saddam's interrogators wielding iron bars. Brig. Ali Sadiq was a charming host but he had a few issues with the former regime and was not likely to be the most open-minded, even-handed man to lead an investigation unit such as this. After we left the facility, being covertly photographed as we did so, we returned to the Green Zone where a hot debrief took place. No one was convinced that we were shown the full facility, the so-called cells we were shown were exactly what they looked like – that is, offices – and we were convinced that there were lower levels to which we were not given access. There was a much darker side to this building and the units which operated from it. I made sure that the UK ambassador was aware of our findings and suspicions.

During the evening of Sunday 15 November, which of course is the first working day of the week in an Islamic country, General Karl Horst, a bald headed, muscular built, kick ass American soldier, led units of his 3rd Infantry Division on a surprise visit to the Bunker which we had been so cordially shown around three weeks earlier. The General and his soldiers found 169 detainees (numbers vary between 169 to 173) of whom 100 showed signs of physical abuse and malnutrition. They were all Sunni Muslims.

The Iraqi reaction was one of concern. Deputy Minister of Interior, Hussein ali Kamal, told Reuters, 'I've never seen such a situation like this during the past two years in Baghdad. This is the worst.' He told CNN, 'I saw signs of physical abuse by brutal beating, one or two detainees were paralysed and some had their skin peeled off.'[18] The Iraqi Prime Minister also expressed concern and instructed his deputy to launch an enquiry. Minister of Interior, Bayan Jabr, however, had a different view. He told PBS America that there were no tortures at the Bunker facility and that those detained were some of the most dangerous criminal terrorists from a number of Arab countries. He confirmed that Engineer Ahmed ran the project and admitted he was a former member of the Badr brigade. Following pressure from the US Ambassador, Zalmay Khalilzad, the US army stepped up its programme of inspections of other MOI installations and uncovered more evidence of the systematic ill treatment of prisoners.

On 29 May 2007, Peter Moore, an IT consultant working from the UK embassy in Baghdad, was kidnapped from the Ministry of Finance building along with his four bodyguards. His abductors were all wearing police uniforms and driving marked police vehicles. He was held for thirty-one months before being released in Baghdad. His four bodyguards were murdered months earlier. There is reason to believe that they fought like the soldiers they were at the end, but they were unarmed and outnumbered. The kidnappers who claimed to be the 'Righteous League' made demands for the withdrawal of British troops and the release of a Shia cleric, Qais al Ghazai, who was being held by the US. Shortly after Peter Moore's release in Baghdad, al Ghazai also obtained his freedom. The Home Secretary, David Miliband, made a public statement that no substantive concessions had been made and Mr Moore's release was due to the process of reconciliation. The Iraqi Minister of Finance at the time of the kidnapping was none other than Bayan Jabr.

Chapter Nineteen
The MOI

Working in the Ministry of Interior day in and day out settled into a routine which, apart from the weight of the body armour, the heat and the thick tobacco smoke and the regular crump of explosions, developed into a sort of normal rhythm. I regularly received 'taskers' from someone in MNSTC-I in the Green Zone asking me to clear up some point or other, usually an administrative issue, with the Deputy Minister such as, why was money for two thousand men being sent to, for example, al Anbar province, when there were only 1,500 policemen on the payroll? Fortunately, to break up the routine I was regularly invited to lunch in the MOI by one Iraqi senior officer or another which would amount to an almighty great gut buster of plates of rice doused in yoghurt (a Saudi tradition I was told) accompanied by spiced lamb and no end of delicacies. The general format was for great cauldrons of food to be delivered which were served up on tin trays and everybody would then help themselves by eating with their fingers from the great variety of dishes spread around the host's office. The great array of food was washed down with cups of warm mud masquerading as coffee served up by a man in traditional Arab dress of dishtasha and shemagh with a tin urn on his back. The only difference between him and traditionally dressed coffee vendors was the shoulder holster and Coalition issued Glock semi-automatic pistol seen peeping out from a fold in his clothes. He only ever carried two earthenware cups around the whole building which were carefully wiped with a cotton cloth before being handed to the next victim. To refuse a drink would have been very bad form. Despite this communal living and intimate eating arrangements, I never suffered a hint of a stomach bug or any other unpleasantness affecting the digestive system. My stomach was clearly up to the job, being the end product of an evolutionary process to which generations of Devon farmers had contributed.

One thing I always considered odd was that, despite the fact that a full on war was going on all around us and dozens and sometimes hundreds of Iraqi civilians, soldiers and police personnel were being killed every day, the MOI stopped working at 3.30pm precisely. By 4pm the building was empty, except for those who slept in their offices and a not insignificant number who spread a blanket on the concrete floor (no carpet) and slept there. It was such a day and time as this, 19 October 2005, a Wednesday, that I left the MOI at 3.30pm to go to the range with my CRG team. I wanted to practise shooting, a skill I needed much practice in and the CRG team wanted the opposite, namely extracting me from a contact with the enemy and getting me to cover as quickly as possible. Half an hour after I got to the range at the police academy situated inside our complex, I received a telephone call from Jane Merryweather, a tall, slim, elegant lady, an Arabic specialist and member of the senior management team at the embassy. She told me that there had been a kidnapping of a *Guardian* reporter called Rory Carroll, who was an Irish citizen and the embassy wanted to do as much as they could to get him freed. She had been unable to get in touch with any of her police contacts, who of course were the same people I interfaced with. She asked if I would go to the MOI and try to find out where they were. Fortunately, I was with my CRG team and Peter Dean, the team leader, a pragmatic man who had already survived one SVBIED attack on his vehicle and sustained facial injuries, authorised the trip immediately. Within ten minutes we were back inside the MOI, which was like a ghost ship save the few men who intended sleeping there that night. I went straight to General Hussein AK's office but it was empty. I tried Major

Abdullah's office and luckily found therein Major Saiff, one of his police colleagues, who thought he knew where Hussein AK was and promised to contact him.

Major Saiff told me that at 3.00pm that afternoon Rory Carroll, who he already knew to be Irish, had been kidnapped from Sadr City whilst visiting friends. I thought this was an odd term as Rory Carroll was a reporter and more than likely to have been following up a story with a journalistic source. He told me that three vehicles had been used in the kidnapping, one of which was a General Motors suburban with IP markings, therefore probably supplied by the US. No one knew where the Irish man was and no demands had been received, as far as he knew.

Within a short while after that, both Hussein AK and Major Abdullah were located and made contact with Ms Merryweather. They were already working on the case and had been visiting the scene of the abduction. I checked back in with her and things at the embassy were whirring so I wasn't needed for the moment. I returned to my accommodation at the FOB where I found Duke watching CNN, a channel he would rarely watch as he called it 'Communist News Network.'

'One of your folks, a reporter, has been kidnapped,' he said.

'I think he's Irish,' I replied. 'That may be his saving grace but our people are on the case.'

I then told Colin what I knew as he was my boss and then had a quiet evening with Duke and the rest of the US and British advisors around a fire pit smoking cigars, a bad habit Duke had got me into. The embassy and the IP were having far from a quiet night and Mr Carroll must have been in acute fear wondering if he was going to be the next person to have his head carved off with a blunt bread knife.

The next morning, I went into the MOI for work as normal and as I pressed through the ground floor lobby to get to the stairs to start my eleven floor painful climb, I noticed the unmistakable face of an Englishman amongst a sea of Iraqis. Stood next to him was Starsky in the form of Major Abdullah. We looked at each other and more by telepathy than anything else walked towards each other.

'He's one of yours,' Abdullah said. 'Come up to my office.'

I nodded, took one more surreptitious glance at the odd man out, turned away and started the ascent to the Major Crime Unit. On my arrival, I was welcomed by Abdullah and the Englishman who introduced himself. I noticed he was wearing covert body armour under his shirt. Abdullah told me that he, the Englishman and a contingent of IP had entered Sadr city overnight and arrested a man colloquially called Abu Allah. Abu in Arabic means 'father of' and of course 'Allah' is Arabic for God, so the literal translation is the Father of God. The arrest had been difficult and dangerous and the police had discharged their weapons to secure their prisoner; their exit had been like greased lightning. I then entered into an inner room in the MCU and could see the reason for the name as an ancient thin man was sat on the floor in full dishtasha and shemagh speaking in quiet tones. With him and engaged in the conversation was an Iraqi general and head of the unit. I could sense this was not an ordinary prisoner and the IP appeared to be treating this old wizened man with some respect. The whole situation appeared delicate and I thought best well left to the Iraqis so I left them to it. I returned later to be told by Abdullah that Abu Allah or Hussein Finjan, I think he was called, had admitted luring Rory Carroll to Sadr City with intent to kidnap him. Negotiations were in an advanced stage to arrange a prisoner swap! The good news is that they did and at about 10pm the following night, Mr Carroll was released back into the sultry air of Baghdad, shaken but not stirred. The Iraqi police had pulled off a magnificent job but no persons were charged with any offences relating to the kidnapping; not ideal maybe, but Mr Carroll was alive. A lot of people worked hard behind the scenes to effect Mr Carroll's release, not least of whom were Jane Merryweather and Sir William Patey. I saw the ambassador shortly after Rory Carroll's release and said something like, 'Well done, sir.' He told me that London had accused him of being too proactive; he made a gesture not commonly associated with that given by a British ambassador and gave a broad grin. I wrote in my diary that night 'what a gritty guy'.

The only sad sequel to this success by many people working in harmony was in mid-March 2006. I met Major Abdullah with Inspector Jo Jones whilst following up enquiries concerning Margaret Hassan. I found him to be very upset because three days earlier two of his friends, Major Saiff and Major Mohammad, had gone into Sadr city on a crime enquiry. This part of the city was run by the Mahdi army and the IP had a local agreement to leave them in charge and the police would go to a 'visitors' office' to effectively get permission to enter. When they walked into the office they had the bad luck to be recognised by one of the suspects involved in the kidnapping of Rory Carroll. Both policemen were abducted, tortured, their faces burnt with blow torches and then shot in the head. Major Abdullah was approaching the limit of his endurance at this time and I recommended to his senior officers that they should take him out of the line, as he badly needed a rest.

In late December 2005, I was just about to enter the dining facility at the FOB or DIFAC as it was called. I was in the process of clearing my weapon (a mandatory process when entering the FOB) which involves dropping the magazine out (essential) and then pulling back the sliding mechanism which feeds bullets into the barrel and ejecting the unfired bullet. The trick is to catch the bullet when it springs out and not scrabble about for it in the sand as I did once or twice to my embarrassment. One of the CRG chaps, a former Para and sergeant in the French Foreign Legion could perform a feat of catching the bullet in his mouth whilst clearing his weapon; he had those sort of pale blue eyes which seemed to oscillate, not the sort of man you would want to be on the wrong side of. Just when I had my gun pointed into the unloading tube which was stuck in a barrel of sand, I heard a loud thump uncomfortably nearby. About fifteen seconds later there was another thump but this time it sounded duller. 'It's probably mortars near the Green Zone,' somebody said. We then all went in and had lunch, which was anything from rib eye steak to some Mexican tongue burning concoction dearly beloved by the Yanks. It was a break from the grind in the MOI.

As we left the DIFAC, we discovered that a suicide bomber

wearing an explosive vest had stood amongst a line of Iraqi police recruits in the police academy which adjoins the FOB and had activated his vest bomb killing many of the recruits. The survivors ran into a 'duck and cover' bunker which is like a rectangular concrete upside down U shape believing a mortar had exploded in their midst. A second suicide vest bomber ran into the bunker and activated his vest whilst standing in the middle of them. The inside of the bunker walls and ceiling were just one mass of tangled flesh and copious amounts of blood. Thirty-three recruits were killed, including about eight women who strangely had peaceful looks on their faces. All that was left of one bomber was his head and feet; the rest had disintegrated. Unfortunately, the post blast forensic examination amounted to piling the bodies and remains into flatbed trucks and taking them to the local morgue, where they were handed over to relatives and buried shortly thereafter. I picked a ball bearing up off the floor. There were hundreds of them, but no one seemed capable of collecting the forensic debris to establish type, pattern and any other clues regarding manufacture of the devices. Bob Lamburne had got his work cut out.

When I returned from leave in early January 2006, Colin Smith told me about how he had survived another double vest suicide bomber attack on the MOI. On this occasion twenty-eight policemen had been killed at a parade by a bomber dressed as a policeman, the second suspect was challenged and then shot, but those who tried to apprehend him were blown up and killed as he activated his bomb in his dying throes. This war has been a criminal waste of good people's lives. Things didn't get any better; on the 22 February I was on one of my routine visits to Deputy Minister Ali Ghalib when I saw him watching the television in his office in a semi-hypnotic state. The pictures were a live feed showing substantial damage to the al Askari Mosque in Samarra; just the walls seemed left standing and smoke could be seen billowing out. This is one of the holiest sites in Shia Islam but also very open to Sunni Moslems. As a result, over the next two weeks, thirty-two mosques were bombed and over 400 people killed. Iraq looked to be on fire with sectarian hatred. Over the next couple of years, the Mosque would again be targeted by fanatics and the same cycle of murder and destruction followed each time.

I believe one of the greatest successes of the UK policing mission, one in which I had absolutely no part, was the operation of a confidential hot line modelled on the Crimestoppers model and given the name TIPs. This was initially set up by a US Marshal John Grinch, who I met in June 2005 and who described to me how it all worked. Colin Smith was seeking new ways of increasing the meaningful contribution the British could make in the whole effort and the US were open to British police intelligence experts working in the TIPs office. In fact, Chief Superintendent Marks took a leading organisational role and Colin purloined a number of former RUC police officers working as contractors for a private security company called Armorgroup, all of whom had served in intelligence during 'the troubles'. These highly skilled former RUC men who referred to themselves as 'The Continuity RUC' (a twist on the name of an IRA terrorist group) brought enormous skill and energy to this unit. They worked alongside Iraqi policemen and dealt with calls coming in from members of the public in and around Baghdad. They trained their interlocutors in the art of criminal intelligence management, grading information, handling informants and all the other skills of this vital business. As a result of their work, numerous lives of Coalition soldiers (mainly US) were saved, IED's recovered and disarmed, weapons seized and even the bodies of murder victims recovered.

Detective Sergeant Bob Perry led the unit in Baghdad. He was another county man from the Hampshire police and former member of the SAS, an extremely tough character with a gruff Portsmouth accent and a generous spirit. He handled the highly sensitive material his unit acquired with strict compliance to the rules and on more than one occasion was leaned on to reveal to very senior US military officers his sources, which he refused to do. Guaranteed anonymity and security for informants is essential in this shadowy world of intelligence. Bob rolled TIPs out in Basra in 2006 with the same success as had been seen in

Baghdad the year before. The whole system had an Iraqi lead and spliced well into the existing IP criminal intelligence system.

The TIPs project was independently assessed by Andrew Shaver of Princetown University in 2016. In his paper *Information and Communication Technologies, Wartime Informing and Insurgent Violence* he states in conclusion: -

> '*Despite considerable effort by Iraqi insurgents to overwhelm the TIPs hotline managed by British forces in the south, the limited but steady stream of credible information to call centre operators appears to have provided British forces with sufficient information to disrupt insurgent activities. While informing through information communication technology channels during the war does not appear to have effected overall insurgent violence, the evidence suggests that it was responsible for significant reduction of indirect fire, in particular IED attacks.*'[19]

The UK police involved in working on the TIPs project can be very proud of their work. The risks they took, which I cannot go into, the dedication they showed and contribution they made to minimising coalition casualties has never been recognised.

I left the mission in May 2006, feeling frustrated at not having done enough. Whilst I owe a lot to the CRG guys who kept me alive, I was stifled by the security blanket and just wished I could have worked under the same conditions as the military. When I vented my feelings of frustration, one US Marine Sergeant said to me, 'Don't get wrapped round the axle, Tony. Iraq will be here long after we've all gone. It's your family that's important.' He was right of course. On one occasion when I had been flying from Basra to Baghdad, a Royal Navy Lynx helicopter going in the opposite direction had been shot down in Basra that same day. My poor wife saw it on the BBC 24-hour live news feed and when I phoned home that evening completely unaware of this event I found her to be grief stricken. She genuinely thought I had been on that helicopter and was dead; she had been sat numbed on the sofa with a blanket wrapped around her and her teeth chattering on a summer's day. She was waiting for a knock on the door, a knock that was sadly being made in other parts of the country. A number of military personnel including a woman soldier had died and the Iraqi insurgents could be seen on TV jumping for joy. My wife, who has thick, long, brown, quite beautiful hair lost it in great tufts and developed bald patches. The families of service personnel, diplomats and aid workers endure a great deal of angst, but it is hardly ever noticed by the greater public or reported on by the media and these families are numbered in the hundreds of thousands. It was mid-May when I got home, the wild yellow irises were flowering in the water meadows through which the river Frome meandered lazily to the sea, the grass was refreshingly green and the sun so mild and English.

Chapter Twenty
Israel Palestine?

On my return home and by way of rewarding myself I set to the task of purchasing a small sailing boat, a gaff-rigged traditional-looking pocket cruiser called a 'Cornish Shrimper'. I sailed her that summer off the Dorset coast and a friend of mine Hugh Maddox, a retired Anglican priest, taught me all he knew about Shrimpers and he knew a lot. However, before I could get too comfortable, I got a call from Tony Rogers, who had been commissioned by the Northern Ireland Office to carry out a review on a series of sexual abuse cases which had occurred at a children's home in Northern Ireland. For the remainder of 2006, I worked with Tony; Keith Akerman, a retired detective chief superintendent and former head of Hampshire CID; and a retired detective superintendent, John Fox, who became a University Professor and lecturer both in the UK and US. The offences occurred in and around Enniskillen in County Fermanagh and involved men in their twenties befriending girls aged thirteen to seventeen who were in the 'care' of the local authority and who lived in a children's home. The men encouraged the girls to engage in sexual acts with a number of older men for money, cigarettes, gifts and other favours. The police had made an effort to deal with the offences but got into difficulties with obtaining evidence from the girls, some of whom were damaged by previous abuse, had psychological problems and one or two of whom were less than truthful. Nonetheless, these girls were rightly classed as children who had experienced emotional difficulties and it should have come as no surprise that they had been chewed up by life.

Difficult though these investigations may be, there are solutions to the problems thrown up in cases of this type and these solutions are not all new. In Bournemouth, when I had been a detective sergeant there, we experienced similar problems in one of our children's homes. Our uniform patrol officers were all aware of the problems and they set about a policy of arresting men seen in the company of the girls from the home late in the evening after the children should have been back in the residence. This is a crime which has been on the statute books for many years and the relevant current legislation is contained Section 49 of the Children Act 1989, which makes it an offence to take a child out of the care and control of someone or authority who has responsibility for them, for example the Social Services Department. It is relatively easy to prove and does not rely on the child to give evidence. Thus, disruption of a more serious crime can be achieved and the perpetrator can be sentenced for up to six months imprisonment. I wasn't sure if this was the case in Northern Ireland, so visited the office of the Director of Prosecutions in Belfast and a senior lawyer confirmed to me that they had the same legislation on their statute books. This offence had not been exploited by the local police who were very adept at dealing with terrorism, but had got out of practise in dealing with more routine policing matters. Don't forget that it was the RUC who lost over three hundred officers during the IRA terrorist insurgency.

There were a number of other reasons why the abuse of these children occurred, but one major problem which the Social Services Department had was this. On a number of occasions, the girls, aged between thirteen to seventeen would insist on going out in the evening dressed inappropriately for their age. The workers in the home tried to stop them but were frequently told to F off. The Care Home Manager also sent letters to the men involved and in reply they entered the home, ripped the letters up and threw them into the faces of the care workers. Whilst this was in fact excellent evidence to show that the men knew the girls were in care, it displayed blatant intimidation of the staff by men who had links to paramilitaries. The care workers had no legal power to exercise a moral influence on the girls by making them remain in the home or stop dressing so provocatively. I suspect that most parents exercise a natural protective authority that comes with parenthood and would not allow their young daughters to place themselves in such positions of vulnerability. The question must be asked, 'Are these damaged children really being looked after in what is called care?' We presented our findings which comprised thirty-four recommendations to senior commanders of the Police Service of Northern Ireland (formerly known as the RUC) in early 2006, but I am afraid that throughout the rest of the UK this pattern of child abuse and lack by the police and other agencies of joining up the dots carried on with sickening regularity.

It was as this review was drawing to a close that my wife received a telephone call from a Nikki Palmer of Jerusalem. I was out at the time but the person said they would ring back. It sounded to me like someone trying to sell double glazing or solar heating so didn't think much about it. At the due time, the same Nikki Palmer phoned back to say that she worked for DFID in Jerusalem and asked me if I was working at the moment. I told her that I was just finishing a review and would be free in February 2007. She told me that DFID were considering deploying a police advisor to an American-led project engaged in security sector reform. She explained that a member of the project was an American colonel by the name of Lance Lane, who had mentioned my name, because he knew me from Iraq and asked, if I were free, could I join the team which was led by an American three star General Keith Dayton working out of the US Consulate in Jerusalem? They needed a civilian police officer to act as a liaison between their organisation and an EU effort, which was training and equipping the Palestinian police, led by a former Hampshire assistant chief constable called Colin Smith. She asked me, 'Do you know him?' I couldn't believe my luck. I knew the main players and was exhilarated to think that I had an opportunity to work in one of the most fascinating countries in the world on a process that was and remains one of the most important to world peace; it seemed that fortune had smiled on me again. I subsequently underwent an interview, got the job and was despatched to Jerusalem in February 2007.

Lieutenant General Keith Dayton had enjoyed a distinguished career in the US army and had been the Defence Attaché in the US embassy in Moscow. He had also spent a fruitless time in Iraq searching for the fabled weapons of mass destruction with a British brigadier who I would later meet called John Deverell. General Dayton was the United States Security Coordinator and his team comprised about fifty US, Canadian and British military officers plus a sprinkling of civilian specialists such as myself. I will refer to this effort as the USSC. This team were undertaking the task of building the Palestinian security forces, excluding the police. In 2007, the US government and its people gave $89 million to train and equip the Palestinian security services which included training courses, infrastructure projects including buildings, the supply of vehicles and much more. They did not supply weapons but did contribute certain lifesaving equipment which I will talk about later. The USSC was fundamental in helping shape the doctrine of the Palestinian security services, ensuring that they operated within the norms of the Universal Declaration on Human Rights; transparency and accountability. The USSC only dealt with the Palestinian Security forces in the West Bank, although they did help in the establishment and procedures at border crossings within Gaza, but this was an off on approach due to the Hamas-led Palestinians launching rockets at civilian areas in Israel. The strategy behind the whole operation was to produce an efficient Palestinian security force which would combat terrorism, particularly that aimed at Israel. By achieving this goal, the government of Israel would gain confidence in the institutions of the Palestinian Authority which would in turn lead to the establishment of the two state solution as agreed in the Oslo Peace Accords of 1993.

The Palestinian civilian police in the West Bank were being assisted in their development by the EU, who called their mission the European Union Co-ordinating Office for Palestinian Police Support or EUPOLCOPPS for short. This mission comprised seventy police officers from European Union countries. They worked from Ramallah on the West Bank and had specific functions around training and equipping the Palestinian police. They made numerous visits to police stations prisons and courts in the West Bank. My job was to toggle between both missions and keep General Dayton informed as to what the Palestinian police and EUPOLCOPPS were engaged on, in return keeping Colin Smith aware of what initiatives the USSC were committed with.

Israel is an ancient country with a rich history which has contributed enormously to the cultural and religious wealth of the world. Unfortunately, since its re-creation two years after the end of the Second World War, there has been little peace. Israel is a small country with a coastline of 170 miles; it is only 12,100 square miles in area which is twice the size of Yorkshire or the same size as Vancouver Island, just over one fifth bigger than New Jersey USA. The population is 7.4 million of which 75 per cent are Jewish, 20 per cent are Arabs and mainly Muslim; between 700,000 to 1,000,000 are of Russian origin. It is in fact a very diverse, modern, industrialised country with an efficient and creative economy. The Palestinian Authority controlled (but occupied) West Bank contains 2.7 million Palestinians of Sunni Muslim and Christian persuasion. It also has an estimated 400,000 Jewish settlers living within its walled-in land. I will omit Gaza from my story as both the EU and US will not deal with Hamas or any of its institutions as it is a prescribed terrorist organisation.

I arrived in Tel Aviv on the afternoon of Monday 5 February 2006. It was cold – I thought it would be hot like Baghdad – and by the time I got to my accommodation, a small Arab hotel called the Adar in East Jerusalem, I had missed tea and supper. I ventured out as I was hungry and found a kind of snack bar and bought something resembling a spam sandwich, but it wasn't pork. Over the next few days, I started to meet the USSC team members. General Dayton's Chief of Staff was Bernt Willand, a six foot six-inch-tall US army colonel, fiercely loyal to the general and the mission. He was of German descent and his father had fought for the German army in the Second World War before the family escaped to America. He outlined the work being carried out by the team which I have already mentioned and he supplied me with copious amounts of material to read. I was to find Bernt a solid, reliable man who enforced a strict discipline on the team which he expected to perform at the highest level; nobody was here for a holiday. He then took me to meet Lt. Gen. Dayton, who was a slim, gaunt man with grey-black hair and piercing eyes. He was of the same mould as Gen. Petraeus, a scholar soldier and of iron character. I remember well the end of week meetings I attended with the whole team, when we would tell the general of events in our areas of responsibility. On one occasion, a civilian expert who had been bought in to fulfil certain tasks tried to bombard him with facts, figures and complicated solutions backed up by documentation thicker than an old-fashioned telephone book. I was lost on the complexities of the proposal when the general peered over his spectacles like a hawk about to swoop and asked some very simple but direct questions. The self-appointed expert was unable to waffle any further and crumbled as his plans were exposed for being built on sand.

I also met with Colonel Lance Lane shortly after I arrived and immediately noticed he was not wearing his dagger as he did in Iraq, but otherwise looked as studious and yet as soldierly as ever. He was also glad to see me and it was not long before we were working together and he was overloading me with 'taskers' which were questions concerning divers matters about the Palestinian police which the European police officers would help me to answer.

I then drove out to Ramallah from Jerusalem, which is of course in the West Bank referred to by the Israelis as Judea and Samaria as in Biblical times. Ramallah is a sprawling conglomeration of houses and businesses, most of which seemed to have been built in the last fifty years. It is a complete muddle of streets and I got lost numerous times before my ageing brain worked it all out. The office of the EUPM comprised a modern building well-staffed, clean and tidy with armed Palestinian police guards at the front. Here I met Colin and his staff officer, Tony Shaw, a retired Metropolitan Police Special Branch man who, like Bernt, was fiercely loyal to his boss. I liked Tony a lot and we became good friends, albeit I likened his role to being a doctor's receptionist determined to shield the great man from me. Colin was his usual boisterous self and took great pains to teach me all about the activities, hopes and aspirations of the mission. As a result of these comfortable arrangements and the confidence we had in each other, I regularly accompanied EUPM advisors on their visits to Palestinian police stations, prisons and headquarters buildings and quickly built up relationships with Palestinian senior commanders. This enabled me to keep General Dayton and the USSC team fully updated with all current organisational and operational matters affecting the Palestinian police. I must say it was a great luxury to be able to travel throughout the West Bank with either British members of the USSC or members of the EUPM. The Americans on the other hand were very restricted in where they went and were obliged to have the type of protection I had in Iraq if they wanted to visit the places to which I routinely went.

The very first thing I needed to establish was what type of legal system the Palestinians operated under. Again, I was fortunate that the EUPM had working for the mission an Austrian judge called Claudia Fenz. As well as being a domestic judge in Austria, she also specialised in international law and she was able to explain to me in detail how the system worked in Palestine, which was the civil law or Napoleonic system as in her own country (and Iraq for that matter). Thus, the role of the prosecutor was very important and it wasn't long before I was meeting with them. Together with Claudia, I visited a number of courts in the West Bank and was able to watch trials in progress. I was also pleased to see Palestinian women judges sitting in courts and their presence was not window dressing for westerners, they possessed and conducted themselves with real authority. I was very impressed with what I found and soon realised that the major problem they faced was freedom of movement, as the West Bank is occupied and they are financially poor and require investment in infrastructure and logistics. The prosecution and defence experienced great difficulties when conducting court proceedings in ensuring that witnesses could attend court. If the witness came from a different part of the West Bank, getting them to court was made extremely difficult because if the person did not have all the right papers, then they would not be able to get through Israeli Defence Force (IDF) checkpoints. This in turn led to huge backlogs in unresolved cases. Even getting prisoners to court suffered from the same problems. The IDF had check points around all major Palestinian cities such as Ramallah, Jenin, Bethlehem and Nablus, thus confining the residents to those areas. Delays at checkpoints were sometimes for lengthy periods, not helped by what I noticed on some occasions as a surly attitude by the IDF towards the local Palestinian population. There didn't seem to be much of a hearts and minds approach. (See map 'effect of closure and permit regime on Palestinian movement').

Claudia also described to me that a tribal form of justice existed in Palestinian society and other Middle Eastern countries which is called Sulha. This is a system of justice which grew up in the Middle East because the societies were and are tribal and there was an absence of state control because so many different conquerors from the Greeks and Romans, the Byzantines, Ottomans and finally to the British had passed through these regions. Sulha involves the heads of different tribes coming together to decide liability and more often than not, to decide the price of blood money or other restitution. From the time I was in Iraq, I remembered a case of a policeman from Basra killing another person and it was through the tribal chiefs that the matter was finally resolved. I recall it involved the tribe from which the policeman came handing over to the tribe whose member was killed, a woman and a Mercedes Benz car to the satisfaction of all. The same kind of incidents occurred in the West Bank and the courts utilised the process of Sulha within the judicial system. It had some elements of conflict resolution, restorative justice and compensation claims as in the UK legal system all rolled into one. The blood money price for killing a man in Palestine in 2007 stood at around $60,000, subject to negotiations.

The senior British army officer working on the USSC team was Colonel William English, a guard's officer with an Oxford English accent, which seems to be the regulation issue to many British military officers. I worked with William a lot on planning matters and we worked together on establishing a strategic concept; that the civilian police should investigate acts of terrorism and the security force being built by the USSC should provide the force protection to enable them to do their job. This was also very much what Colin Smith thought and as both he and William had worked in Northern Ireland they understood the concept better than most. Both William and I managed to sell the concept to Lance Lane and finally we, with Colin Smith, presented our doctrine to the senior management and it became a part of the overall strategy of the USSC. There was also a tendency for the Palestinian security forces overall to bring people charged with terrorist related or politically motivated crimes before military courts. One senior political advisor who came out from Washington thought this wasn't so bad because it was efficient. The trouble is that such a process lacks transparency; justice must not only be *done*, it must be seen to be done. I informed General Dayton of my concern at the overuse of military courts. He understood my disquiet and set things in motion at political level to change it.

The mission was joined by Brigadier Deverell, who I met for the first time at a meeting in the British Consulate in Jerusalem on Friday 11 January 2008. The consulate in East Jerusalem deals with the Palestinian Authority, the embassy in Tel Aviv deals with the Government of Israel. I noticed that the brigadier was resplendent in what appeared to be a Second World War battledress plus a cravat in the colours of Eton. He was about six feet three inches tall with a strong, gaunt face and black hair, but didn't seem to be wearing socks. He had a noticeably high forehead which was clearly to house his enormous brain. An accomplished soldier and excellent leader, he had come to join the USSC and was intent on establishing a staff college based on the Sandhurst model for the Palestinian security services (all of them) based in Jericho. In order to do so, he needed a budget which he found and additional staff to work there. He spoke fluent Arabic and I was lucky to go with him one weekend to the ancient and abandoned city of the Samaritans on the top of Mount Gerizim above Nablus. It is here that the Samaritans believed that God ordered the building of a temple, not in Jerusalem and they were subsequently ostracised by the Jews. The ruined city is spectacular and deserted, as is Sebaste nearby. Mount Gerizim is one of the highest in Israel at 2849 feet. From the summit, you can see the Mediterranean Sea to the west and the mountains of Jordan to the east. Israel is very narrow at this point and was nearly cut in half during the Yom Kippur war by armoured forces from Iraq, but they failed to exploit their advantage and were destroyed by the IDF. Strategic vulnerabilities such as this are a big worry for the IDF and compound their insecurities. Unfortunately, Israeli citizens are prohibited from entering large parts of the West Bank and tourists appear to avoid Nablus (also the site of Jacob's well) as it is said to be infiltrated by Hamas. The tourist potential for much of Palestine is enormous and could bring huge benefit to the local people, but very few visit. When John and I went, we only had to encounter a profusion of Palestinian hospitality and were offered more fruit juice by residents than would be needed to float a battleship. I was exhausted in the heat of the climb and when we arrived at the top of the mountain, I had trouble getting my ageing body across a dry moat into the City, but the brigadier had already clambered sprightly across and hauled me over with one hand.

In 2007, the US Congress voted the USSC £89 million dollars to train and equip the Palestinian security forces. The mission comprised a number of logisticians whose job it was to supply the equipment needed and obtain the consent of the government of Israel to import, transport and deliver the material. A routine job one may think, but not in Israel. Every item of equipment was picked over, questioned and in many cases rejected. The USSC ordered 150 Dodge trucks for the Palestinians but the Israeli civil servants would not allow them to be supplied as the windows did not meet European Union specifications, not that Israel is in the EU and they were not going to be used in Israel anyway, but this delay took months of negotiations to resolve. When the Palestinians finally got them, one of their officers made the complaint that they were 'gas guzzlers' and they could not afford to run them. It would be nice to please some of the people some of the time but on occasions we could not please any of the people any of the time.

Colin's mission EUPOLCOPPS also had problems in supplying the Palestinian police with equipment with the same nit-picking delays. Two French gendarmes were involved in training the Palestinians in riot control and had been trying to deliver hundreds of public order protective helmets to the police. They could not understand why the Israelis would not allow the equipment through which had been held up for over six months. Fortunately, Brigadier Deverell had established a good rapport with the IDF West Bank Commander and I was aware that he had arranged a meeting with him; I asked to tag along to try to break this log jam. After the formal meeting had been concluded, I managed to include in the 'any other business' section of the meeting my concern about the public order helmets. The IDF general was of the belief that they were bullet-proof helmets, I took great pains to explain that they were made of a toughened plastic designed to protect against stones and bricks not bullets. I am glad to say that I could see recognition in the Israeli general's eyes and within a week we got authorisation to supply the police with the helmets. The representatives of the government of Israel were very wary about equipment which was being supplied to the Palestinian Authority and concerned that it could be used as weaponry against Israel. The possibility of Palestinian security forces being issued with body armour by the USSC was almost an impossibility to negotiate. One can occasionally see conspiracy theories of deliberate obstruction, but sometimes civilian civil servants and their military counterparts do not always join up the dots, which I believe may well have been the case on many occasions. Once again, this demonstrates that foreign missions are very much about establishing relationships and maintaining integrity.

I have been privileged to attend several Shabbat dinners with lovely Jewish families who were some of the nicest people I have ever met and I met correspondingly courteous and charming Palestinian families. It is such a great pity that so much enmity exists between peoples who have far more in common with each other than anybody else. I dealt frequently with a former Islamic Jihad member turned peace worker, who frequently referred to the Jews as his cousins. But this is a region of contrasts and on one occasion I was driving back to my accommodation when I sharply cut in-front of a car, having just carried out some atrocious driving and I was clearly in the wrong. The car behind me then overtook, cut me up and all five men in the car, Orthodox Jews with large hats and bushy beards, all shook their fists at me. It was my fault, but I would have not expected such deeply religious people to be quite so aggressive. When I parked the car by my apartment on the edge of East Jerusalem, two Palestinian boys aged about six hid behind a car and as I walked along the pavement past them, they fired their toy Kalashnikov guns at me which had flashing barrels. One was wearing a green bandana with Arabic writing on and they both shouted, 'Infidel Allah Akbar.' What a crazy country I thought.

My work with the USSC was largely at a strategic level and I carried out a lot of visits and assessments of Palestinian security procedures and facilities. The USSC by its name also co-ordinated security sector aid from other nations so that the whole operation had great cohesion. Many nations contributed in helping the professional development of the Palestinian Authority and its institutions. However, it was not all quite so routine. On Thursday, 4 December 2008, Joe Walker Cousins, a highly educated Arabic speaker and one of Brigadier Deverell's team within the USSC, together with a couple of other specialists like myself, made what was a regular business trip to Jenin. This city is situated at the northern end of the West Bank and adjoins Israel in the area of Nazareth which has a high density population of Israeli Arabs. General Dayton was pursuing a project, in which Joe was heavily involved, trying to normalise the border crossing from Jenin into Israel and for Israeli Arabs to pass easily into

Jenin. This is a highly fertile area where large amounts of vegetables and fruit are produced. The relaxation of restrictions at the border would lead to greater volumes of Israeli Arabs coming into the city of Jenin, buying goods and leading to an upsurge in commerce which would be good for everyone. What the Israelis wanted to know was, would their security be compromised? I had regularly visited and was well acquainted with the Palestinian police commander for the area and had made a number of visits to the local prison; however, today was to be different.

We called on Colonel Abu Asidi at the security forces base in Jenin after a drive of an hour and a half. We were greeted with the usual Palestinian courtesy and glass cups of chai – no milk again, as in Iraq – and discussed operational matters and lines of communication between his units and the forces of the IDF, plus some other security issues. After an hour or so, we left to travel to Nablus in the south, which is roughly in the middle of the West Bank. We there met the governor, who told us about local arrangements that had been made for the relaxation of check points around his city for the period of Eid, which was that coming Sunday. Hotel bookings and obviously restaurant bookings were all up from the previous year and there was a positive sign of improvement. Unfortunately, it was not to last.

We set out for Jerusalem in a buoyant frame of mind, when, just as we drove towards the checkpoint out of the city, we were met by the mother of all traffic jams. Cars were skewed this way and that and appeared to have flooded into an area the size of a football field. Joe was driving and made a skilful job of weaving in and out of the chaos until we could get off the road and engage our four-wheel drive. We were in a Land Rover Discovery, but, as is the way with sod's law, it was un-armoured. We usually used an armoured vehicle for this trip but they had all been taken. As we skirted the rough ground to the IDF checkpoint, we could see the cause of the problem. About a dozen Palestinian private cars were abandoned with their windscreens and side windows broken and a mob of Israeli settlers were throwing rocks at anything Palestinian. Joe managed to drive us off the rough ground through the abandoned cars and as we thought we were free, a crowd of settler women wearing headscarves, long thick woollen dresses and long woollen socks tried to throw themselves in front of our car. Just to our right and by sheer chance, I saw our Canadian friends from the USSC including Mike English, a great burly Ranger, trying to gently move his vehicle forward with about two or three settler women hanging on to his windscreen wipers. We had more speed than the Canadians and Joe exploited a gap, drove through and we were away, but we couldn't go on and leave the Canadians behind. I called up Mike on our radio and asked where was he and did he want us back to help?

'No, Tony, it's alright,' he replied. 'We're coming up behind you now; we just stopped to date a couple of local girls!'

This was all said in a casual manner and, knowing him, with a roughish grin; I guess he had seen worse. But our excitement was not over just yet. As we approached the ancient town of Shilo, the road was on fire in front of us. Settlers had put burning tyres across the main road to Jerusalem and were emerging from the thick black smoke wearing ski masks and whirling sling shots around their heads, David and Goliath style. It was no moment for indecision and I said, 'Just punch through, Joe,' and he drove through the fire and we emerged onto a clear road with the Canadians right behind us. Despite several sling shots being loosed in our direction, they skimmed over our roof but didn't hit us; they lacked the skills of their ancestor the shepherd boy, David. Apart from a demonstration that had just petered out near the entrance to Ramallah and with the IDF deploying in force, things quietened down. The events had been sparked off when a group of settlers in Hebron in the southern West Bank, the burial place of Abraham and under a split Palestinian-Israeli control, had been evicted from a house they were occupying illegally in the Palestinian area. The settlers had purchased the house from a Palestinian family, no doubt for a hefty sum, but Israeli citizens were not permitted by the government of Israel to buy houses in that Palestinian area. The judgement given by the Israeli court was upholding international agreements in place for Hebron and ensuring that they were adhered to by its own people.

It was between May and June of that year that the Palestinian Authority Security Forces carried out 'Operation Hope,' which was widely reported to be a success. It was later independently commented that 'the streets have been mostly cleared of illegal weapons and cars and armed gangs can no longer roam the streets openly.'[20] Following this success, the government of Israel permitted further operations by the armed security forces of the Palestinian Authority in other parts of the West Bank including the hotspot of Hebron.

I concluded the mission a week later and returned again to the tranquillity and security of Dorset. One can be critical of the government of Israel but it must be remembered that we are not surrounded in the United Kingdom by millions of fanatics and nation states with an avowed wish to rub us off the face of the earth. It has happened before and the motto of the IDF (and all Jewish people) is 'never again'.

Conclusion

I had spent eight years since my retirement either on foreign missions, training for the missions or awaiting postings. In the gaps I was very fortunate to be involved with some interesting major crime reviews. I had neglected my wife, my family and my house which was in need of much repair. I also had a Cornish Shrimper that had been under-used and I knew a retired country parson who had time on his hands, something I would have thought that he would have been used to. So after some strenuous work as a builder's labourer and general dog's body, the house was brought up to standard, my wife started to get used to me again and the Reverend Hugh Maddox and I bent the Shrimper into the wind on some exciting sailing.

I can't remember the date when I received the next phone call; I had stopped keeping a diary. It was the FCO. They had just the job for me, the police head of criminal intelligence in Afghanistan needed an interlocutor and help with the British policing model of information handling. This was the only war zone in the first decade of the twenty-first century I hadn't been to. I just needed approval from my Three Star General Judith, who was listening to the phone call and I saw her face fall. I couldn't do it to her again, I couldn't face any more tears and it was my fault her hair fell out the last time. It took one look and I said, 'Thanks, but no thanks.' I never got any more telephone calls.

It was with enormous pride that on 9 June 2010 that, together with Judith, son James and daughter Catherine, I attended Buckingham Palace where I was awarded the MBE by the queen for services to international policing, more recently in Iraq, Israel and Palestine. It was the proudest day of my life.

I am afraid there are many loose ends which remain, Margaret Hassan lies in an unmarked grave in or around Baghdad. The killers of Brian Tilley never faced justice, bar one who faces a higher authority. True detective stories unfortunately reflect life which is far from perfect. I have been very fortunate (that word again) in working with some of the finest detectives and police officers not only in Dorset, but from all over the world. I have also been privileged to meet with some enormously brave people such as Marinko Durcevic, the state prosecutor of Bosnia and Herzegovina; Major Abdullah; Captain Amir of the Iraqi Police Service and many more. I have worked amidst intellectual giants such as Brigadier Deverell, Sir William Patey, and General Dayton; good fortune has remained with me throughout. Most of all I owe my wife Judith everything, who for years was on her own at home and had much worry without a great deal of support. My guidance and inspiration came from God.

Notes

Chapter 3

1 NATO led Stabilisation Force deployed between 1 January 1996 to 31 December 2005.

Chapter 4

2 Adam D. (2004) Science. 'What is Red Mercury'. The Guardian [online] 30 September 2004. Available from www.theguardian.com/science/2004/sep/30/this weeks sciencequestions1.

Chapter 6

3 UN Human Rights Chamber for Bosnia (1996) Josip Bozana and Tomislav Matanovic Against The Republika Srbska. Ch/96/1 dated 13 September 1996. Bosnia and Herzegovina Human Rights Chamber. Available from http://www.unhcr.org/refworld/docid/3ae6b67024.htm

4 Bosnia and Herzegovina Country Reports on Human Rights Practices. *US Dept of State* [Online] March 4 2002. Available from www.state.gov/j/drl/ris/hrrpt/2001/eur/8236.htm

5 The Right to Know: Families Still in the Dark in the Balkans. (2012) Amnesty International August 2012 EUR 05/001/2012. *Amnesty International* Pages 1 – 16. Available from: www.amnesty.org/eng/documents/euro5/001/2012/en

Chapter 7

6 United Nations (2000) Protocol to Prevent Suppress and Punish Trafficking in Persons, Especially Women and Children, Supplementing The United Nations Convention Against Transnational Organised Crime. United Nations Article 3 Paragraph (a) Page 2. Available from: www.osce.org/odihr/19223?download=true

7   United Nations Protection Force February 1992 to March 1995.

Chapter 8

8   Cockburn A. (2003) 21st Century Slaves. *National Geographic magazine* September 2003 pages 2 – 24.

9   Organised crime is the collaboration of two or more persons, for a prolonged or indefinite period of time, in the commission of serious criminal offences, which are determined by the pursuit of profit and or power. Members usually have defined tasks. The group usually has a hierarchal structure, uses violence or threats of violence to intimidate members of the group and maintains discipline and control. Groups of this nature exert influence including corruption over the police; politicians; and judiciary. Based on the definition used by the *Bundeskriminalamt* or BKA (German State Crime Police).

Chapter 9

10   Biography de Laverne Celhia www.stopinternational.org img.pr.com/release-file/0910/184811/STOPCelhiadeLav

Chapter 16

11   SCIRI is the acronym for the Supreme Council for the Islamic Revolution in Iraq, also known as the Supreme Assembly of the Islamic Revolution in Iraq (SAIRI). It was founded in Iran in 1982 by Ayatollah Muhammad Baqr Al Hakim and other Iraqi Shia Muslims as a resistance organization devoted to overthrowing Saddam Hussein and instituting an Islamic republic in Iraq.

12   I have extracted the details of the court case from Howard M. and Campbell D. (2006) The Guardian. [Online] 5 June 2006. Available from: www.theguardian.com/uk/2006/june/06/world.iraq

13   O'Doherty C. (2013) Seeking Justice for murdered Margaret Hassan. Irish Examiner. [Online] 1 January 2013. Available from: www.irishexaminer.com/ireland/seeking-justicefor-murdered-margaret-hassan-218239.html

14   These figures are much debated but counts of deaths reported in newspapers are collated by groups like the Iraq Body Count project. They estimate that 174,000 Iraqis were reported killed between 2003 and 2013, with between 112,000-123,000 of those killed being civilian non-combatants.

15   Joint statement from the FCO and MPS on the kidnapping of Margaret Hassan. Undated and unsigned and not on any form of headed paper.

16   R V Oliphant 1905 2KB67 is one of a number of cases which allow criminal acts in other countries to be dealt with in English law where the impact is felt in England or Wales. Certain offences of terrorism and child abuse are also specifically catered for. See cps.gov.uk/legalh-tok-/jurisdiction/#an03

Chapter 18

17 See Jakub Cerny (June 2006) 'Death Squad Operations in Iraq' 06/28 [Online] published by Defence Academy of the UK Conflict Studies ISBN 1-905058. Available from studies.agentura.ru/centres/csrg/death.pdf

18 Wilson J. 173 Prisoners found beaten and starved in Iraq bunker. 'The Guardian' [online] 16th November 2005. Available from www.theguardian.com/world/2005/nov/16/usa.iraq

Chapter 19

19 Shaver Andrew (April 2016) *'Information and Communication Technologies, Wartime Informing and Insurgent Violence'*. [Online] Households in Conflict Network, University of Sussex. Page 41. http://www.hicn.org/wordpress/wp-content/uploads/2012/06/HiCN-WP-215.pdf

Chapter 20

20 Zanotti Jim (2010). US Security Assistance to the Palestinian Authority. Congressional Research Service. [Online] Available from fas.org/sgp/crs/Mideast/R40664.pdf

Index

Many Arabic names are prefixed with al, such as al Jazeera. I have therefore chosen to group all Arabic names with this prefix under 'A', in the hope of avoiding any confusion.